Who the Hell is Immanuel Kant?

Who the hell is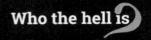

For students, teachers and curious minds, our **carefully structured jargon-free series** helps you really get to grips with brilliant intellectuals and their inherently complex theories.

Written in an **accessible and engaging** way, each book takes you through the **life and influences** of these brilliant intellectuals, before taking a deep dive into three of their **key theories in plain English.**

Smart thinking made easy!

POLITICS   PSYCHOLOGY   PHILOSOPHY   SOCIOLOGY   ART HISTORY

Who the Hell is Immanuel Kant?

And what are his theories all about?

Dr Mark Robson

BOWDEN
&BRAZIL

First published in Great Britain in 2021 by
Bowden & Brazil Ltd
Felixstowe, Suffolk, UK.

British Library Cataloguing-in-Publication Data
A CIP record for this book is available from The British Library.

Series editor & academic advisor: Dr. Jonathan C.P. Birch, University of Glasgow.

ISBN 978-1-8382286-3-7

To find out more about other books and authors in this series,
visit www.whothehellis.co.uk

Contents

Introduction

Immanuel Kant (1724–1804) is, without doubt, one of the greatest thinkers of all time. Indeed, such has been his influence and the profound extent of his legacy, that many thinkers talk in terms of 'before Kant' and 'after Kant'. He is regarded as having made some avenues of thought no longer navigable. The eminent German theologian, Karl Barth (1886–1968), for example, talks of Kant as a 'stumbling block and rock of offence in the new age […] a prophet whom almost everyone must reinterpret before they can do anything' (quoted in Chigwell, 2009). His philosophical depth and wideness of vision divides Western intellectual history into two.

Kant inaugurated a 'Copernican revolution' in philosophy which extends to all areas of thought. This revolution is alive and well in the ways we think, regard the world and, most important of all, in how we act. If anyone is serious about understanding one of the cornerstones of current thought in morality, science, mathematics, art, theology and philosophy, a study of Kant is absolutely indispensable.

Kant could have had a minor role in the history of thought were it not for the famous Scottish sceptic, David Hume (1711–1776). In his late fifties, Kant read about Hume's philosophy and this reading kindled a spark within him which became a mighty conflagration in Kant's mind. It created a veritable storm of writing as Kant tried to battle the raging conceptual fires within him. In one intense decade Kant produced work of such brilliance that it can only be described as astonishing. One of the most learned historians of German thought, Lewis Beck (1913–97), says this, 'I know of no decade in the life of any philosopher which even approaches this one in the quantity, variety, and importance of what Kant did in these nine years [1781–1790].' (Beck, 1969)

The three (late) great works we will concentrate our attention upon are *Critique of Pure Reason* (1781), *Critique of Practical Reason* (1788), and *Critique of Judgement* (1790). They are often referred to as the first, second and third *Critiques*. It is these works which divide Western intellectual history into before and after Kant.

In the first *Critique* Kant tries to map out the real extent of our reasoning powers. What can the human mind do, and what are its limits? Hume had argued that we should be sceptical about human intellectual powers. Kant tried to address this scepticism and to show what we could be certain about. In the second *Critique* he asks how we should behave in the light of the conclusions of the first *Critique*. What should be the source of our actions? Are we really free to act, or are we more like robots who inevitably obey the laws of physics? In the final *Critique*, the one which Kant sees as bringing all his ideas together, he tries to answer any remaining questions left over from the other *Critiques*. He particularly tries to look upon the idea of beauty. What is this elusive concept, and how can we judge something as being beautiful?

These three great works are generally regarded as being amongst the most difficult books in the history of thought. However, the aim of this book is to get to the heart of Kant's philosophy, without getting caught up in scholarly disputes over the interpretation of his innovations. We will also avoid discussing the critical reaction to Kant's ideas. This is to keep the explanations as clear and as uncluttered as possible. In the conclusion, we will then briefly examine some criticisms of Kant's ideas, so the reader knows something about the problems in Kant's philosophy.

Kant's ideas are exciting, revolutionary, and inspiring. They are difficult, but certainly not impossible to understand, and when understood they invigorate the mind and bring fresh insights into the ways we think.

1. Kant's Life Story

Emanuel Kant was born on the 22 April 1724 in the city of Königsberg. Situated on the south-east corner of the Baltic Sea, Königsberg was part of German East Prussia up until 1946, when it was renamed Kaliningrad after its annexation by the Soviet Union. Meaning 'King's Mountain', Königsberg would go on to develop into an important intellectual and cultural city and Kant lived there all his life.

A Morally Decent Upbringing

The son of Johann Georg Kant (1683–1746) and Anna Regina Kant, née Reuter (1697–1737), Emanuel was the fourth of nine children, although only five survived, leaving him as the eldest. Emanuel, or Immanuel as he would later call himself, is from the Hebrew לְאוּנְמָע, meaning 'God with us', a name which Kant was always proud of and apparently considered most appropriate. Kant's father was a master harness maker, originally from Tilsit which was just over 40 miles from Königsberg, and his mother was the daughter of a master harness maker in Königsberg. Anna Regina was well educated compared to many women of that time, having a flair for writing and a love for nature. Marrying Anna allowed Johann to join the guild, something that would have been all but impossible for an outsider. Being a member of the guild meant the family were considered to belong to the 'respectable' classes with an element of social standing and respect, even though they were never wealthy. After the death of his father-in-law, Johann was forced to move his family to live with his mother-in-law, which was in a less profitable location. Having now to compete for business with local saddle makers (who were allowed to make harnesses), as well as being affected by problems within the guild system itself, it was not easy for Johann to provide for his family. But provide he did. Both he and Anna must have done a good job in caring for their children as Kant was always full of praise for them, writing in a letter later on in his life that

> *'my two parents (from the class of tradesmen) were perfectly honest, morally decent, and orderly. They did not leave me a fortune (but neither did they leave me any debts). Moreover, they gave me an education that could not have been better when considered from the moral point of view. Every time I think of this I am touched by feelings of the highest gratitude.'* (Kuehn, 2001)

The Kants lived just outside of the city in an area that was both residential and commercial, with warehouses, pubs and boarding houses. Their street was busy and noisy and their neighbours were fellow harness makers and saddle makers, whose children Emanuel played with. Königsberg was actually very multicultural with many Lithuanians, Mennonites from Holland and Huguenots from France. There were also Poles, Russians, a large Jewish community and Dutch and English merchants, all

Fig. 1 Königsberg, East Prussia (now Kaliningrad, Russia).

living in close proximity and dealing with one another through business, if not necessarily mixing socially. Growing up in these rather cosmopolitan surroundings, Kant would have become accustomed to a variety of different cultures.

The Influence of Religion

Both of Kant's parents were devout members of the Pietist movement within the German Lutheran Church. Pietism was very influential on German social and cultural life. It taught that faith should be more than church going or bare adherence to a set of doctrinal statements – it should be a faith which expresses itself in loving action and private prayer. Social and educational concerns were part of the loving action that the Church held in such high esteem, with charity channelled into orphanages and schools for the poor. It was this element of Pietism that influenced Johann and Anna Regina. Pietism also insisted that hard work was a sacred duty and that the conscience of each individual was supreme. Certainly the emphasis on hard work and the importance of the inner voice of morality would be a major influence upon Kant throughout his life.

However, Pietism wasn't accepted by everyone in Königsberg. The orthodox clergy, the city administration and the faculty of theology at the university were all strongly opposed to the movement. This conflict between a 'religion of the heart' and the more traditional society in Königsberg would, to a certain extent, play out in Kant's own life, as we will see.

A Slave to School

When Emanuel was eight-years old, his intelligence was recognized by one of the pastors at the local church and he was enrolled at the *Collegium* – a Pietist school that aimed to not only embed Christianity into children at an early age, but also to instruct them in the humanities as this was felt to be good for their wellbeing, making them more 'worldly'. This was a good opportunity for Emanuel to advance himself socially but it came at a cost. The school schedule was gruelling with lessons beginning at seven o'clock and ending at four in the afternoon, six days a week with few holidays. His evenings would be taken up with homework and on Sundays, his only day off, he was obliged to attend church with catechetical exercises afterwards.

Lessons consisted primarily of Latin, which was considered to be the most important discipline, and was taught alongside theology, Greek, Hebrew, mathematics, religion and the history of philosophy. Emanuel excelled at Latin and developed a love for the ancients, which he would continue to read well into old-age. He also discovered what would become a life-long passion for

Fig. 2 Friedrichs-Collegium, Königsberg.

classical poetry. It is often remarked that Kant's tastes in the arts were very narrow as he had no appreciation of music and was indifferent to paintings and sculpture. But this is hardly surprising with a regimen as strict as the students of the *Collegium*.

Although the school itself was rather dark and dull, it provided a sound education. A school friend corresponded later about their experiences saying that 'thirty years have passed since the two of us groaned beneath the pedantically gloomy, but not entirely worthless discipline of those fanatics' (quoted in Scruton, 1997). Whatever the merits of the school, Kant emerged from it with great self-discipline and the capacity to work extremely hard.

A Death and a Rejection of Pietism

In 1735, the same year that Emanuel's grandmother died, Anna Regina gave birth to the last of her children, a son who she named Johann Heinrich. Sadly, only two years later at the age of 40, Anna died, exhausted by multiple pregnancies, caring for her family and nursing a dying friend. Emanuel was only 13 at the time and was devastated by the death of his mother. He is quoted as saying

> *'I will never forget my mother, for she implanted and nurtured in me the first germ of goodness; she opened my heart to the impressions of nature; she awakened and furthered my concepts, and her doctrines have had a continual and beneficial influence in my life.'*
> (Kuehn, 2001)

Whereas before, Kant could at least look forward to the happiness and warmth of his family when he arrived home from school, now he returned home to sorrow and grief. Being a member of the guild, Kant's father Johann was thankfully well supported. He also received help from family members and

Fig. 3 University of Königsberg, commonly known as 'The Albertina'.

friends and Anna Regina's brother funded Emanuel's studies, allowing him to complete his final three years.

The *Collegium* had prepared Kant well for further studies in theology, the classics, philosophy or law, although many of the students were expected to take up a career in the Lutheran Church. A Pietist education set out to instil total obedience to orthodox religious practice, even deeming it 'necessary to break the natural willfulness of the child' (Kuehn, 2001). But for Kant, this was entirely objectionable. The Pietists believed that our human will is influenced by a form of the supernatural which meant they rejected moral autonomy. But, as will become apparent in his thinking in later chapters, Kant sought to justify autonomous morality through his belief in our freedom of will.

Even though both his homelife and school life were based upon religion, and indeed both were Pietistic, the contrast could not have been more different. At home, he received love, encouragement and acceptance while at school he was forced to conform and any natural temperament that didn't align with the strict way of life of a Pietist was immediately suppressed. It appears to be the effort of his teachers to convert and 'break' the young Emanuel, that caused his aversion to many aspects of religion.

The Albertina

Kant was accepted at the University of Königsberg, commonly known as the Albertina, in September 1740 at the age of 16. The change that his life underwent was radical. For the first time, he was allowed to study any subject he wanted and had the freedom to spend his days as he wished. Kant's uncle continued to support him but he lived frugally nonetheless and earned money by tutoring other students, with whom he garnered quite a following. He was serious about his studies, foregoing a lot of the frivolities that the other students involved themselves with, but he did have a penchant for billiards and also the card game *l'hombre*, both of which he played extremely well, and also for money. According to Kant playing cards 'cultivates us, makes us even-tempered, and it teaches us to keep our emotions in check. In this way it can have an influence on our morality' (Kant quoted in Kuehn, 2001).

The philosophy at Königsberg University had moved on from being solely Aristotelian in its orientation (although this still played a large part) and the principles of Gottfried Leibniz (1646–1716) and Christian Wolff (1679–1754) were now considered important. However, much in the way that the Pietists were gaining support in the city, they also began to gain a foothold at the university with the king's backing. Wolff was declared an atheist (although an atheist at that time could mean little more than not toeing the confessional line) and his texts were banned for a while, threatening freedom of philosophical expression.

Not long before Kant entered the university, Franz Albert Schulz (1692–1763) arrived in Königsberg. Professor of Divinity and a Pietist, Schulz nevertheless had a mediating effect on how philosophy was taught at the Albertina, believing that theology and philosophy should be taught together. Having been a student of Wolff, Schulz reinstated his philosophy on the curriculum and so, on entering the university, Kant studied a mixture of Pietist theology and Wolffian philosophy.

Towards the end of 1744, Kant's father suffered a stroke. This was to have profound implications for Kant who, being the eldest, was now responsible for his siblings, the youngest being only nine years old. His new responsibilities restricted his freedom to study and go to all his lectures. It is thought that he spent much of 1745 at home working on his first book *Thoughts on the True Estimation of Living Forces* (1747). Johann Georg Kant died the following year in 1746, shortly before Kant's twenty-second birthday.

Entering the Workforce

Having graduated in 1748 at the age of 24, Kant left Königsberg for the first time to take up a string of posts as a private tutor. Although he always claimed never to have enjoyed his role as a private tutor and considered himself to have been bad at it, he must have made a good impression on his employers as he was popular among the families he worked for and he stayed in contact with them. It was during this time that he honed his social skills and polished his manners in polite society. According to one of his biographers, Borowski, it was also during this period that he penned ideas for some of his later works (Kuehn, 2001).

Determined to go back to Königsberg and take up a position at the university, Kant returned in 1754 to prepare his dissertation. He also began work on his second major oeuvre as well as writing a series of essays. Kant handed in his finished dissertation, titled 'Succinct Meditations on Fire', in April 1755, receiving his doctorate. However, to be able to teach, Kant had to first write and defend a second dissertation. His submission, 'New Exposition of the First Principles of Metaphysical Knowledge', argued that Leibniz and Wolff's basic principles (the principle

Fig. 4 Immanuel Kant (1724–1804)

of contradiction and the principle of sufficient reason) are not the very *first* principles. He offered instead a system which he called 'the system of the universal connection of substances' (Kuehn, 2001).

Kant succeeded in getting a position at the university as a private docent or lecturer. The post was unsalaried but docents were able to earn money by charging students fees for attending their lectures and also by giving private tuition. Kant lectured on maths, logic, metaphysics and physics, later adding geography and ethics. He based his lectures on the philosophy of Leibniz and Wolff and by all accounts his lectures were popular right from the beginning with students fighting for space. He was known for his dry humour and poker face and his classes had the reputation of being lively, witty and enjoyable.

Over the next few years, Kant's standing grew with offers of professorial posts arriving from several German universities including a very prestigious university post in Berlin. But Kant was no lover of travel (during his entire life his longest journey from Königsberg was one trip to Arnsdorf – a journey of just 60 miles). So Kant remained in his post as lecturer at Königsberg University and waited patiently until eventually, in 1770, he was offered a professorship in logic and metaphysics. It was now that Kant concentrated more of his attention on philosophical questions.

A Person of Elegance

Having been very adept at living well, albeit frugally, Kant's new position eased his financial burdens considerably. Kant was an attractive man who took great care of his appearance. With blonde hair and striking blue eyes, a slender build and an elegant taste in clothes, Kant stood out from his more sombre, clerical colleagues. According to his biographer, Manfred Kuehn (2001), Kant

> 'always followed [...] the "maxim" that the colors of one's dress should follow the flowers. "Nature does not create anything that does not please the eye; the colors it puts together always fit precisely with each other." Accordingly, a brown coat required a yellow vest.'

Mixing with nobility, Kant was a regular dinner guest of the Count and Countess Keyserlingk. But he never forgot his roots and was friends with people from all social classes. In fact, the republican ideals that make up his political writings are clearly based on his own background. He disliked pretentiousness and felt that 'a philosopher might be more at home in a farmer's pub than among distorted heads and hearts' (Kant quoted in Kuehn, 2001).

Although Kant never married, and is often painted as having had little interest in women, he did in fact have a number of relationships. Whether they were intimate is not known, but on two occasions it appears that he was considering marriage. One was a young girl from Westphalia with whom he spent some time in society but, by the time he thought to propose, she had returned home. The second was a beautiful widow who came to Königsberg to visit relatives and with whom Kant is thought to have wanted to share his life. But it seems that 'he calculated income and expenses and delayed the decision from one day to the next' by which time she married someone else (Kuehn, 2001). It would appear that his ever-practical nature was not to be persuaded by his heart.

An Engaging Professor

Kant's lectures continued to be popular. Students had to be there an hour early at six in the morning to make sure of a place. One of his pupils reports that Kant's lectures were a master class in careful methodical thought and that they were sometimes extremely moving especially when he was speaking about morality.

> *'In these [lectures] he ceased to be merely a speculative philosopher and became, at the same time, a spirited orator, sweeping the heart and emotions along with him [...] How often he moved us to tears, how often he stirred our hearts to their depths, how often he lifted up our minds and emotions from the shackles of self-seeking egoism to the exalted self-awareness of pure free-will, to absolute obedience to the laws of reason and to the exalted sense of duty to others!'* (quoted in Scruton, 1982)

Kant strongly believed that appreciating elegance and beauty in nature and literature were of greater importance than just reading and learning from books. He wanted to teach his students to think for themselves: 'You will not learn from me philosophy, but philosophizing, not thoughts merely for repetition but thinking' (Kuehn, 2001). Kant was very European in his outlook, striving to be a man of letters, reading and applying the ideas of English and French authors, as well as his fellow German writers. In this way, too, he differed from his university colleagues.

From Excess to Moderation

When Kant was in his thirties, he was a central figure in the social circles of Königsberg. After finishing his lectures in the morning, Kant would meet friends for lunch and then go directly on to a coffee house where he would continue socializing as well as sometimes playing billiards. His evenings were spent dining with friends and acquaintances, often not returning home until after midnight and not always steady on his feet.

However, in 1764 when Kant turned 40, his life underwent quite significant changes. He withdrew from his thriving social life and underwent something of a 'mid-life crisis'. He lost some of his closest friends which affected him greatly. It was around this time that Kant returned to considering the psychology of character – a theme he had included in his lectures on anthropology. Kant believed that we are not born with our character but that it is something that we acquire, and not before the age of 40. He says:

> *'It is like a kind of rebirth, like a certain solemn kind of promise to oneself. [...] There will perhaps only be few who have tried to accomplish this revolution before the thirtieth year and even fewer who have firmly founded it before they are forty.'* (quoted in Kuehn, 2001)

The kind of 'rebirth' that Kant was referring to was not just a rebirth of character but also of morality: by following the moral law, we gain dignity and self-mastery through the ability to govern ourselves by the application of rational principles.

Being physically delicate, Kant suffered from mild scoliosis, weak and under-developed muscles and a delicate bone structure. He was therefore always careful not to overexert himself and was forever attentive to his body. He was also prone to worry and anxiety. When Kant experienced his 'rebirth' in his fortieth year, he gave himself the advice of 'constant occupation of the mind, to take a great deal of exercise, and to live moderately, especially to shun drinking at night' (Kuehn, 2001). The result was a more moderate Kant whose philosophy was about to enter a new stage.

A More Mature Philosophy

Kant's new appreciation of maxims was not only due to his wish to live a more moral life and to overcome his weak physical condition, but it was also due to valuable new friendships. One in particular was with a highly esteemed merchant called Joseph Green – an Englishman who had come to Königsberg when he was young. Green lived his life by strict rules in a most pedantic fashion, following the hours of the clock religiously. Kant and Green became very close with Kant gradually embracing Green's way of life.

Focusing his mind on his new maxims, each of Kant's days ran to a tight schedule, almost never varying. He was woken at five o'clock by a servant when he began work at his desk dressed in robe, night dress and cap until his lectures began at seven when he donned his lecturing clothes. When he finished

Fig. 5 *Kant and Friends at Table* by Emil Doerstling, 1892.

his lectures at eleven he would redress in his night clothes and again work at his desk with concentrated attention. At one o'clock he would take lunch. This was the social time of Kant's day and there would be guests, each of whom would be given a pint of claret. This time of witty repartee and entertainment would last until three o'clock when Kant would take his walk around Königsberg. Whereas before he enjoyed the company of friends, now he always walked alone. It is said that Kant's afternoon walk was so regular that people could set their watches to his schedule around the city. Reputedly the one time the routine was broken is when Kant lost himself in reading Jean Jacques Rousseau's *Émile* (1762). (Rousseau's ideas, as we shall see in Chapter 2, were a major influence upon Kant.) The rest of the afternoon would more often than not be spent with a visit to Green who promptly ended the evening at seven o'clock sharp, when Kant would leave for home.

Unlike many of the merchants in Königsberg, Green was a very learned man, preferring to read books than conduct business. Both he and Kant shared the same principles and loved to read and discuss Hume and Rousseau (1712–1778). According to Kant's friend Kraus, 'The association with the highly original and most righteous Englishman Green assuredly had not just a small influence on Kant's ways of thinking and especially on his study of English authors' (Kuehn, 2001).

The Silent Decade

From around 1773 there was what has become known as the 'silent decade' where Kant continued to lecture but published almost nothing. He was working hard on his ideas which were largely a response to the scepticism of the Scottish philosopher David Hume whose relentless questioning Kant famously said awoke him from his 'dogmatic slumbers'. Kant pondered, wrote and pondered anew trying to show that we could have real, rationally founded knowledge of the world (see Chapter 3).

It was from this point on that Kant's lecture style changed. Where once his students had considered him to be entertaining and engaging, now his lectures were obscure and difficult to understand. A couple of years after the publication of his *Critique of Pure Reason* in 1783 (the first of his most influential works), Kant was obliged to defend himself against allegations that he had written the book in an abstruse language that made it impossible to comprehend his philosophy. In a letter to fellow philosopher Christian Garve (1742–1798), Kant explained:

> *'the expression of my ideas – ideas that I had been working out painstakingly for more than twelve years*

in succession — was not worked out sufficiently to be generally understandable. To achieve that I would have needed a few more years instead of the four or five months I took to complete the book.' (quoted in Kuehn, 2001)

Despite this, Kant's *Critique of Pure Reason* established him a lasting reputation as one of the world's greatest philosophers. But there were two more works of similar philosophical importance and magnitude — *Critique of Practical Reason* and *Critique of Judgement.* These works are so revolutionary and important that scholars distinguish two periods of Kant's academic career. The three *Critiques* are Kant of the *critical* period. Works before that are seen as *pre-critical* Kant. In this book we will examine Kant's work of the critical period.

The Declining Years

Preparing for his final years as his health and mental powers began to decline, Kant finally bought himself a house in 1783 at

Fig. 6 Kant's house, now a ruin in Kaliningrad, Russia.

the age of 59. While he never diverted from his strict routine, he continued to invite friends and acquaintances to lunch right up until his last few years of life. One of his lunch guests, Friedrich Lupin, reported

> *'I have seen only few men at his age who were so lively and agile as he was [...] It was one of the characteristics of this great man that his deep thinking did not stand in the way of his cheerful socializing. He was all pure reason and deep understanding, but he did not burden either himself or others with it.'* (quoted in Kuehn, 2001)

At the university, the philosophical faculty had taken on a more Kantian outlook, something that Kant had actively been working towards throughout his time there. He gave his last lecture in 1796, and over the next few years his mental and physical faculties slowly declined to the point where he was longing to leave the world. Immanuel Kant died on the 12 February 1804. His last words were *'es ist gut'* (it is good). His tomb in Königsberg has a quotation inscribed on it which is taken from the end of his second *Critique*:

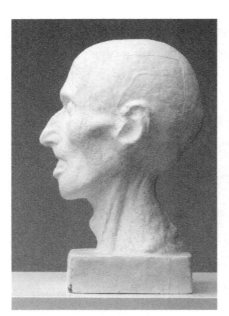

Fig. 7 Kant's deathmask, created in 1804.

'Two things fill the heart with renewed and

increasing awe and reverence, the more often and more steadily we meditate upon them: the starry firmament above and the moral law within.'

These words are well-chosen. When we study Kant's philosophy, we shall see that he thought that the moral law is something we have to give ourselves, and that nature, at its most awesome, reminds us that humans are special beings of incomparable worth and dignity.

Immanuel Kant's Timeline

Kant	World Events
	1712 Frederick II (the Great), future King of Prussia is born
1724 Kant is born 22nd of April	
1732 -40 Attends Pietist school *Collegium Fridericianum*	**1735** Jonathan Edwards leads a protestant revival in the USA, The Great Awakening
1737 Death of mother, Anna Regina née Reuter	**1739** Hume publishes *Treatise of Human Nature*
1740 Enrols at University of Königsberg	**1740** Frederick II becomes King of Prussia
1746 Graduates from university; death of father, Johann Georg	**1745** Battle of Hohenfriedberg – Frederick the Great's army defeat Austria and Saxony
1747 Publishes first philosophical work *Thoughts on the True Estimation of Living Forces*	
1748 -55 Works as a tutor to various families	**1748** Discovery of the Ancient Roman town of Pompeii
	1752 Benjamin Franklin flies a kite to show the electrical nature of lightning
1755 Graduates with Master's degree and appointed unsalaried lecturer at University of Königsberg	**1755** Great Lisbon earthquake impacts Portugal
1765 Meets English merchant Joseph Green (1727–1786)	**1763** Treaty of Hubertusburg ends the war between Prussia, Austria and Saxony
	1769 Captain Cook reaches New Zealand
1770 Appointed as Chair of Logic and Metaphysics	**1770** The slave triangle controlled from Liverpool ships millions of Africans across the Atlantic
	1773 Boston Tea Party

	1776 American Declaration of Independence
1781 Publishes *Critique of Pure Reason*	
1783 Publishes *Prolegomena to any Future Metaphysic which shall lay Claim to being Scientific*	
1785 Publishes *Groundwork of the Metaphysics of Morals*	
1786 Death of Joseph Green	1786 Frederick the Great dies
1787 Publishes second Edition of *Critique of Pure Reason*	
1788 Publishes *Critique of Practical Reason*	
	1789 George Washington elected first president of the United States; French Revolution and the Storming of the Bastille
1790 Publishes *Critique of Judgement*	1790 Edmund Burke publishes his critical *Reflections on the Revolution in France*
	1792 Louis XVI is guillotined
	1793 The Terror in France begins with 3000 people being executed in December
1796 Stops lecturing	
	1800 President John Adams moves into the newly completed White House
1801 Retires from Professorship	
1803 Kant's sister Catharina Barbara (1731–1807) moves in to care for Kant	
1804 Kant dies February 12th	1804 Napoleon has himself proclaimed Emperor of France

2. Influences on Kant's Thinking

There is evidence of the origins of Kant's thought reaching right back to his childhood. As he went through life, his parents, teachers, colleagues and friends all had an effect on the direction his thinking went. In this chapter we will trace that trajectory, paying particular attention to those great minds that had a marked effect on his later thought – his critical philosophy – as this will give context to his most important theories that are covered in the following chapters.

The Importance of Moral Values

As we saw in the previous chapter, Kant's childhood was very much centred around religion, both at home and at school. However, while one source proved a positive influence on Kant's thought, the other would steer Kant in the opposite direction.

The Pietism that Kant's parents practised instilled in their son a sense of duty, self-worth and confidence, and above all, strong moral values. Their own self-determination and self-sufficiency and their sense of honour was very much a characteristic of life within the guilds. It is this that they passed on to Kant. The Pietism that Kant experienced through the church and through his strict schooling, however, demanded submissiveness and obedience to a higher authority, whereas for Kant 'moral culture must be based on maxims not on discipline'. He believed that 'the representation of right lies deep in the soul of everyone' and that one should lead 'the child to ask: "Is this the right thing to do?" rather than telling it: "You should be ashamed of yourself"' (Kant quoted in Kuehn, 2001). We see the importance of this separating of morality and religion in Kant's *Metaphysics of Morals* (1797).

Philosophers of Old and New

Kant was taught by tutors of differing beliefs and philosophies who largely fell into one of two camps: the Pietist–Aristotelians and the Wolffian–Leibnizians. However, like many of his contemporaries, Kant remained an independent thinker. He took from each what he found valuable as we can see in his *Metaphysics of Morals*, when he says: 'it is thought improper not to defend the ancients, who can be regarded as our teachers, from all attacks, accusations, and disdain, insofar as this is possible.' Yet it is 'a foolish mistake to attribute pre-eminence in talents and good will to the ancients in preference to the moderns just because of their antiquity.'

There are traces of Kant's thinking in many of the teachings of his tutors. Three in particular are perhaps worth a mention: the first is Kypke, a Pietist whose work persuaded Kant of the distinction between synthetic and analytic that would play an important part in his *Critique of Pure Reason*. Another Pietist, Johann Gottfried Teske (1704–1772), who taught Kant theoretical and experimental physics, formed his student's views on the nature of electricity and fire, and on which Kant wrote his first dissertation. A third is Martin Knutzen (1713–1751) – one of the most influential philosophers at Konigsberg who was a Pietist in the Schulzian fashion and therefore taught Wolffian philosophy, although was not averse to criticizing Wolff's principles. It is thought that he had a great influence on Kant and, according to Kant's student and biographer Borowski, he was one of Kant's favourite teachers. Kant's friend Kraus (Kuehn, 2001) claimed that it was Knutzen's *Rational Thoughts on the Comets* (1744) that sparked Kant's interest in science and led to his work *Universal Natural History and Theory of the Heavens* (1755).

Pre-critical Period

However, prior to 1769 it is difficult to pinpoint any specific influences on Kant's early philosophy, other than those already discussed, as he was deeply sceptical of all philosophical theories and 'not attached to anything'. His scepticism can then perhaps be seen as part of his method leading up to his critical philosophy. As he says in his *Critique of Pure Reason*, the 'first step in matters of pure reason, marking its infancy, is *dogmatic*. The second step is *sceptical*; and indicates that experience has rendered our judgement wiser and more circumspect' (1781). And thus we can assume that his final step is his *critical* philosophy. Kant's thinking on metaphysics, morality, and his understanding of beauty have quite distinct influences, which we look at in some detail.

Background to Kant's Understanding of Reality

Kant's thoughts about the nature of reality emerge largely as a response to two great, but very different thinkers, Gottfried Wilhelm Leibniz (1646–1716) and David Hume (1711–1776).

Leibniz thinks that reason can find a way to sure and certain knowledge while Hume emphasizes the role of experience. As might be expected, they come to radically different conclusions, and it is Kant's genius that finds a way between the two kinds of philosophy that brings out the best in both.

The Problem of Objective Knowledge

The problem Leibniz and Hume address is that of objective knowledge. It is important to appreciate what this problem is in order to understand how and why Kant approached it in the way he did. The problem comes as a response to these kinds of questions: What knowledge do we have? What knowledge are we capable of attaining? How can we truly know?

We seem to have knowledge of what goes on inside our own minds, and we can, it appears, directly observe our own thoughts and feelings. This kind of *subjective*, personal knowledge does not seem to be a problem. Surely if we have a pain or think of a shade of blue, we have knowledge that this is what we are experiencing. There does not seem to be any room for error. Why is this kind of knowledge apparently so easy to attain? The answer is that there doesn't appear to be any gap between *seeming* and *being* when it comes to our own subjective experiences. What *seems* to be the case *is* the case when we experience something in the inner citadel of our minds.

This is in stark contrast with the *objective* knowledge that is the concern of both Leibniz and Hume (and eventually Kant). Here what seems to be the case does not have to be the case. There is a looming and unavoidable gap between seeming and being. For example, we may seem to see a sheep in the field but that does not guarantee that we are right. It may be a poodle instead. Or it may be a weird practical joke and someone has cunningly disguised a rock as a sheep!

The problem of *objective* knowledge is the problem of what goes on *outside* our self, beyond the inner workings of our own psychology. The problem comes, in other words, when we go out from ourselves and attempt to state an objective claim. The question is then: can there be objective knowledge of tables and chairs as well as the subjective knowledge of pains and other internal mental items?

René Descartes

The great French philosopher René Descartes (1596–1650) had shown, in a startlingly vivid way, that this kind of external, objective knowledge is extremely difficult to obtain. In his famous *Meditations* (1641), he uses the fiction of an all-powerful Evil Demon who, Descartes supposes, is doing his utmost to deceive him. The table that you see and you think of as an objective, external item could be a Demon-inspired figment of your imagination. This page you read right now and judge to be outside yourself could be another piece of Demon-inspired trickery, and the information it contains wholly false. With the possibility of such a Demon, all our objective knowledge turns to dust. Descartes employs this hypothesis to see if anything

Fig. 8 René Descartes (1596–1650)

Fig. 9 David Hume (1711–76)

can survive a really radical purge of doubt. If it can, then it is truly certain. Only from such sure, indubitable foundations can any kind of proper science be built.

Descartes tried to negotiate his way out of this threat of scepticism by starting from subjective certainty, especially the certainty of his own existence (the famous *Cogito ergo sum*, 'I think, therefore, I am') and from there he used an elaborate series of arguments which tried to show, using pure logic, that there must be an external, objective world. If he had succeeded, then the problem of objective knowledge would have been solved. Unfortunately not many have been convinced by Descartes' approach. Can we have objective knowledge then? Can we have knowledge that there are tables and chairs? Can we construct a science that gives us knowledge of the external world?

Hume's Answer to the Problem of Objective Knowledge

Let us briefly examine Hume's approach to this problem. Hume tries to emulate a hero of the Enlightenment, Isaac Newton (1642–1727) by proposing that Newton's experimental method that had proved so successful in the study of the motions of bodies be directed towards the inner workings of the human mind. If we direct our thoughts inward and carefully examine our experiences perhaps we can find a way to knowledge.

Hume proposes that any claim to knowledge must be rooted in experience. We cannot go beyond the bounds of our own experience since if we do so we do not really know what we are talking about. 'Every idea is copied from some preceding impression or sentiment; and where we cannot find an impression, we may be certain that there is no idea.' (1748) All our ideas – anything we can think meaningfully about – must have its origin in some prior impression.

By an impression Hume means an experience. He notes, by way of example, that a blind person has no way of really knowing what blue is like since the sensory organs which allow that experience do not work. The person who is mild and meek in temperament does not really know what anger feels like on the inside, and cannot understand the rage of the intemperate. The mind, when confronted by an experience which either comes by way of the five outer senses or our internal impressions (say, of anger or pain), retains a faint copy of the experience. This idea is added to our store of ideas. From this storehouse, furnished solely by the actions of experience, we build more complex ideas.

In the 19th century those philosophers who emphasized the role of experience became known as the empiricists. This kind of empirical philosophy became the principal thought pattern of much of Europe and America. Unfortunately Hume found that his empirical method was not a strong enough foundation to secure objective knowledge as he could not prove that there even is an external world, let alone any knowledge about it. A careful examination of experience reveals that all we ever actually experience is one thing happening and then in the next moment another thing. The supposed causal link is invisible to the senses. The best thing to do, he concludes, is to rely on our senses and the habits we have built up over the years.

Leibniz's Answer to the Problem of Objective Knowledge

Leibniz's philosophy is very different. He does not see experience as our best way to knowledge. Reason, he thinks, will provide a surer path. It is significant that many of the philosophers who put reason rather than experience at the centre were mathematicians. (Leibniz is the discoverer, along with Newton, of the immensely powerful differential calculus.)

The rationalists noted that, in the area of mathematics, we find the most objective certainty. Their paradigm was geometry. We can *prove* Pythagoras' Theorem for example therefore, it seems there can be no room for doubt. In the thought world of mathematics, it seems that careful reasoning leads to knowledge. Perhaps the careful, methodical application of reason can lead us towards objective knowledge of the world itself.

If we look at one of Leibniz's arguments we can appreciate his methodology. For example, can we prove God's existence? Relying wholly on our experiences would not appear to be reliable enough. To put this in the jargon of philosophers, working from or after experience, or *a posteriori*, is too unreliable. Instead, we have to work *a priori* – that is, from ideas alone or prior to experience. Leibniz thinks we can prove God's existence just working from the idea of God being the most perfect being. To do this, Leibniz employs his version of Descartes' Ontological Argument, an argument originally put forward by Anselm of Canterbury (1033–1109).

Basically the argument says that existence is a perfect-making property. It is, after all, better to exist than not to exist. A non-existent God certainly cannot be omnipotent and omniscient. Such a God would hardly be perfect! Surely, however, a good definition of God is a being who has *all* perfections, and if existence is a perfection, then God must have that as well. Hence it follows that God must exist.

Leibniz goes on to argue that the idea of God is of a being who is so perfect that His existence would not be

Fig. 10 Gottfried Wilhelm Leibniz (1646–1716)

due to chance or dependent upon circumstance, but is absolutely necessary. After all, how could a being who only *happened* to exist really be the most perfect being? No, God must, if He exists, be a necessary being, unlike our human existence which is far too chancy and contingent.

Leibniz now examines whether the overall idea of God is coherent or not. If it is incoherent, then, like a round square, God's existence is not even possible. Leibniz finds, at least to his own satisfaction, that God's existence is possible since the idea is not incoherent. Therefore we can have certainty about the existence of God, and hence we can have objective knowledge.

Whatever we think of such an argument, it illustrates Leibniz's *a priori* rationalist methodology – relying on reason alone to get to objective conclusions about the nature of reality. Like Descartes, he thinks that it is possible for the human mind, with the correct use of reason, to draw safe and certain conclusions about what the objective world must be like.

How Kant Responds

Kant's genius is to find what is valuable in both approaches. He also finds a revolutionary way of combining them. He is especially concerned with Hume's scepticism. Do we really need to give up the quest for objective knowledge of an external world? He agrees with Hume that, without experience, there cannot be any knowledge at all, but he also agrees with Leibniz that experience is not enough to provide the certainty that we want from genuine knowledge.

Is there, then, an ingenious way to combine reason with experience, and somehow emerge from the enclosed world of inner subjective certainty to an objective, external world? Kant thinks that we can if we realize that experience is not the simple thing that Hume and the other empiricists thought it to be. Our ideas are not just *copies* of the impressions that impose themselves upon us. We both receive *and make* the impressions and experiences that come to us from the supposed outer world. The world impresses itself, but we contribute to the shapes those impressions make. Each experience that you have is, according to Kant, a mixture of the raw, unshaped inputs from the senses and the moulding character of the mind. But the details of that remarkable thought can wait until the next chapter.

Background to Kant's Ethics

Kant reports that it was Jean-Jacques Rousseau's writings that led him to a new understanding of the moral worth of each individual. Rousseau argued that the history of humanity's existence had been one of decline. Civilization, instead of being the saviour of mankind, had really been its enslaver. The person of the modern world is not more free but less free than the people of the remote past.

Rousseau does not recommend that we destroy civilization and return to the woods and, as he puts it, live with the bears. The reality is

Fig. 11 Jean-Jacques Rousseau (1712–78)

that we live in the modern, civilized world, so what is the best way to gain freedom without the absurd step of destroying society? Can we find a way to make ourselves as free as possible within the confining boundaries of civilized society?

Free Will

One of the primary ingredients of freedom is our ability to choose. This ability, says Rousseau, is one of the distinguishing marks that makes us more than mere beasts. Animals, we suppose, are led by whatever happens to be the strongest desire at any one moment. If a dog desires food, it will eat. It will not consider the implications of this and the consequences for its health. Humans, however, are different. We are remarkable in our ability to consider the options. As Rousseau writes in his *Discourse on the Origin of Inequality* (1755):

'It is not so much the understanding that constitutes the specific difference between the man and the brute, as the human quality of freedom [...] and it is particularly in his consciousness of this liberty that the spirituality of the soul is displayed. For physics may explain in some degree the mechanism of the senses and the formation of ideas; but in the power of willing or rather of choosing, and in the feeling of this power, nothing is to be found but acts which are purely spiritual and wholly inexplicable by the laws of mechanism.'

And again in 1762 in his treatise on education, *Émile*, Rousseau says,

'My will is independent of my senses; I consent or I resist, I am defeated or I conquer [...] I have always the power to will, not the force to execute. When I yield to temptation, I am acting under the compulsion of external objects. When I reproach myself for this weakness, I am listening only to my will [...]'

Rousseau is saying that human beings have a will that is almost 'magical' or supernatural in its ability to defy the laws of nature. We can drive ourselves from within rather than always being led by outside influences. In other words, we can be spontaneous or original. As we shall see in Chapter 4, Kant also thinks that human beings have the extraordinary ability to defy or transcend the laws of mechanism. We are not clockwork beings but radically free, and it is this freedom that confers on us a unique and incomparable dignity.

The General Will

This emphasis on choice leads Rousseau into one of his most famous ideas – the notion of the general will. When a body of people come together in order to form a general consensus on certain matters, they have a collective will that is directed towards the purposes of their society. In this way, we can talk about the 'will' of that body of people almost as if they have become a single conscious, responsible being. The more general the will (the larger the group), the more it becomes, not just the voice of an individual or group, but the voice of the whole. In this way it also becomes more just. In his *Discourse on Political Economy* (1755), Rousseau even identifies it with the voice of God: 'the most general will is always the most just also, and the voice of the people is in fact the voice of God.'

This idea is developed further in what is perhaps his most influential work, *The Social Contract* (1762). Obviously there will be times when the will of the people will conflict with individual wills. How then are we to be as free as possible while at the same time being sometimes forced to conform to the general will? Rousseau puts the problem like this:

> '*How to find a form of association that will, with the whole common force, defend and protect the person and good of each associate, and through which each individual, while uniting with all, will nevertheless obey himself alone and remain as free as possible.*' (1762)

One idea that Rousseau rejected was that we *give up* our individual will for the sake of the security that a larger body of people can provide for the individual. Instead, with his 'social contract', he proposes a way of preserving the maximum amount of freedom while enjoying the liberties and advantages of societal living:

> *'What man loses through the social contract is his natural liberty, and a limitless right to all that tempts him and that he can reach. What he wins is civil liberty and ownership of all that he possesses.'* (1762)

Indeed, Rousseau argues that every time we conform our will to the general will, we are more free. In one of the most notorious passages of *The Social Contract* he writes that if we are impelled to conform to the general will we are being 'forced to be free'. The general will of the people knows more since it is the universal voice, not just the expression of one individual. It knows when you are entangling yourself in knots, and unties them for you thus enabling you to escape your self-imposed confinement. For Rousseau, who saw society as being unjust and unequal, forcing us to be free is an act of compassion; a way of liberating us from our own selfish and destructive ways. We gain so much and lose so little.

But even more importantly, he says, we can, through this kind of give and take association with others, come to possess a 'moral liberty', which alone makes man truly master of himself; for the impulsion of mere appetite is slavery, while *obedience to the law you have set yourself is liberty.'* (1762) (Author's italics.)

This emphasis on the power of the universal or general will had a profound influence on Kant's conception of ethics, especially the notion that it is through obedience to the overall will that you obey yourself (and which we can recognize in Kant's obedience to his maxims – see Chapter 1). Kant will say, in the spirit of

Rousseau, that to conform to the universal law is not to be a slave, but to free yourself since you are no longer bound by your personal appetites and desires like a beast. You become one with humanity's universal voice or will, and in obeying the call of this voice, you discover you are really obeying yourself.

Background to Kant's Theory of Beauty

In Kant's day, philosophical questions about the nature of beauty became known as aesthetics. In the *Critique of Judgement* Kant asks what conditions are necessary to have a true judgement of taste.

The history of the philosophy of beauty or aesthetics is, of course, complicated, and Kant's views are a very involved and nuanced result of these reflections. There is, however, one writer who Kant, in the *Critique of Judgement*, mentions as one of the greatest of writers on aesthetics, and that is Edmund Burke (1729–1797).

Burke is known primarily for his political views, and is often seen as the father of modern conservativism. His *Reflections on the Revolution in France* (1790) was hugely influential and continues to be so. However, much earlier than this Burke had published the work that Kant so greatly admired: *A Philosophical Enquiry into the Origin of our Ideas of the Sublime and the Beautiful* (1757).

Fig. 12 Edmund Burke (1729–97)

The Beautiful and the Sublime

The distinction between the sublime and the beautiful goes back at least to the writer Longinus (early first century CE). The idea was that some things are so astonishingly beautiful that they become sublime. It is this kind of usage that we have retained in ordinary talk. For example, we might say that a brilliant footballer scored a 'sublime goal' meaning that the shot was astonishingly beautiful in its unerring accuracy. Here we mean that the sublime is a kind of beauty, but taken to an extreme degree.

However, for Burke the beautiful and the sublime are very different kinds of reactions which arise from very different kinds of stimulus. The sublime cannot be beautiful. The beautiful cannot be sublime. For example, the beauty of a rose is very different from the breath-taking sight of a tremendous cliff or a raging storm. The rose is gentle, small, and gives pure pleasure, while our thrill in the cliff or storm is mixed with fear and apprehension, which is part of the delight. Therefore, says Burke, a rose is beautiful but a cliff or a storm is sublime.

The Properties of the Sublime

Burke tries to uncover what it is that makes us react in these different ways. What are the rules or principles which govern these areas? He says that the sublime produces astonishment: 'The passion caused by the great and sublime in nature, when those causes operate most powerfully, is Astonishment, and astonishment is that state of the soul, in which all its motions are suspended, with some degree of horror.' (Burke, 1757) This astonishment is often accompanied by terror and fear, which resembles pain in its discomforting effects. So what makes things terrible?

Burke tries to list the typical properties that elicit feelings of fear and terror in the spectator. It seems that what terrifies us is dark or obscure in some way:

> 'To make anything very terrible, obscurity seems in general to be necessary. When we know the full extent of any danger, when we can accustom our eyes to it, a great deal of the apprehension vanishes. Everyone will be sensible of this, who considers how greatly night adds to our dread, in all cases of danger, and how much the notions of ghosts and goblins, of which none can form clear ideas, affect minds [...]' (1757)

For example, many people reported that once they had seen the shark in the film *Jaws* (1975), they felt less dread. In the first parts of the film, the shark's awesome presence is only hinted at by the brilliant music score, and it is this brooding obscurity that enlarges the sense of fear and terror.

Burke says that there is another property which gives feelings of dread and apprehension, and that is great power. The storm is, of course, one example. To this list Burke adds vacuity, darkness, solitude and silence, which he calls privations. Then there is vastness like the mountain or the ocean. All these things can terrify, but when they are experienced in a certain way the discomfort can also give delight. He says,

> 'When danger or pain press too nearly, they are incapable of giving delight, and are simply terrible; but at certain distances, and with certain modifications, they may be, and are delightful as we every day experience.' (1757)

In other words, we are thrilled when there is danger, but only when it is modified by a kind of distance. People go on roller coasters to seek the thrill of the sublime. They are seeking the delight in what gives fear and apprehension when they really know that they are safe.

Kant's Interpretation

As we shall see in the final chapter, Kant agrees with Burke on a number of points. He, too, thinks that beauty and sublimity are very different from each other, and that sublimity requires a certain distance: close proximity to a storm or a raging torrent would be too terrifying. He also agrees with Burke on another point. Burke says that feelings of sublimity are greater in their effect upon us than feelings about the beautiful. Beautiful things are typically small, smooth and are not abrupt, angular or sudden. Instead we have gradual variation. These things give us pleasure, but the kind of pleasurable delight that the storm gives us is far greater in its effect. This is due, he thinks, to the fact that pain is a far greater thing than pleasure in its effect upon us. (Would we, he says, choose a life of great pleasure if we knew that we would be slowly tortured to death at the end of it?)

Kant agrees that the sublime is greater in its effect upon us, but the reasons he gives are very different. The beautiful makes us feel part of the world in a way that is safe and comforting. Whereas the sublime reminds us that we belong ultimately to a different dimension of existence altogether.

Burke tries to trace what it is about the properties of the beautiful and the sublime that gives us pleasure or delight. In the end, he concludes that both reactions are due to the nature of our bodies. The smoothness of the beautiful relaxes the fibres of our bodies. It is gentle, relaxing, and our bodies and eyes are calmed. The sublime, on the other hand, is delightful because it exercises and so flushes out encumbrances and blockages in the body. There is a curious combination of exercise/tension and subsequent relaxation since we are not actually endangered. Burke calls it a 'tranquillity tinged with terror' (1757).

Kant thinks all this is fine, but not deep enough for a truly philosophical explanation. Bodily explanations of the feelings of sublimity and beauty do not, he thinks, get to the core of the matter. They are too 'physiological'. We will explore all these fascinating thoughts in Chapter 5.

As we shall see, again and again as we study Kant, he is constantly seeking for the *necessary* conditions which govern things, and the nature of the body and its fibres cannot provide these kinds of necessitating grounds.

3. What Can We Know?

Kant's greatest work in metaphysics is his famous and ground-breaking *Critique of Pure Reason*, which was published in 1781 and then extensively revised in 1787. The work was so revolutionary, and the investigations that it conducts are so difficult, that it took Kant a whole decade to write it. Indeed, this time is often known as the 'silent decade' such was the concentrated intensity and single-mindedness of Kant's efforts.

The book is universally regarded as one of the most difficult and challenging ever written. Kant himself realized this and published a short summary of its main ideas and arguments in 1783, entitled *Prolegomena to any Future Metaphysic that Shall Come Forth as Scientific*. (In Kant's time, the term 'science' referred to any kind of objective knowledge. It had not yet narrowed its meaning (in the English speaking world at least) to mean physics and chemistry and the like.) Most people read the *Prolegomena* before they embark upon the *Critique*.

The *Critique's* Main Aims and Objectives

Let us start with a short summary of the aims of the *Critique* to get an overall idea of what Kant is trying to achieve. The *Critique* has two principal aims:

1. It aims to show that we can have real objective knowledge of the world and, in particular, that reason can arrive at judgements that apply to the necessary structures of reality. This is the rationalist aspect of Kant's metaphysics as mentioned in Chapter 2. Kant calls knowledge about the structures of reality 'synthetic *a priori*' and says that the main task of metaphysics is the question, 'How is this kind of knowledge possible?' We will unpack what all this means below.

2. The book also aims to show the *limits* of our metaphysical knowledge. Here Kant wants philosophers to be more modest in their ambitions because, he argues, we cannot have knowledge about those things which we cannot experience with our senses. This means that, strictly speaking, we can have no knowledge about God and the immortality of the soul as well as the freedom of the will. None of these things are open to sensory examination. Kant calls reasoning about such things 'speculative metaphysics' and rejects it unless it can be justified on *practical* grounds. We cannot have knowledge of God by the use of pure reason alone. Instead belief in God is a practical requirement for the yet-to-come and hoped-for moral perfecting of the world. Kant famously said that, in this kind of area, he had to 'deny knowledge in order to make room for faith' (1787). The emphasis here is upon the importance of sensory information and as such represents the empiricist aspect of Kant's philosophy.

Let us first look at what Kant means by the notion of the synthetic *a priori*, the most important part of his metaphysics.

Types of Judgement: *a priori* and *a posteriori*

To see what is involved in Kant's view of judgement, we have to understand his innovative technical terminology. Although the word '*a priori*' was commonly used (as well as its opposite *a posteriori*), the distinction between the analytic and the synthetic was largely Kant's invention. (We can find precedents for it in the history of philosophy, but the terms, as Kant uses them, are a definite break from the past.)

If something is known *a priori* it is known independently of experience. Let's take the claim 'All triangles have three angles'. Although we need some initial input from experience to know that triangles have three angles, the claim has a subsequent independence from experience. If you study mathematics you will go further and deduce that a triangle's internal angles must add up to two right angles (180 degrees). The knowledge that all triangles must have three angles and must add up to two right angles is not something that might change and is not dependent upon experience. It is an *a priori* judgement – one that Kant says is 'absolutely independent of all experience' (1787).

But if we look at another claim, such as 'The daffodil is yellow', we require information from the senses to know what colour daffodils are (or at least have someone tell us about it, which of course would be sensory information too). If no one has ever seen daffodils or had any kind of sensory information about them, we can hardly say that the daffodil related claim has any right to be called knowledge.

This sensory kind of knowledge is called *a posteriori* – it comes after (posterior to) the senses. Crucially, the claim *continues* to rely on the senses. After all, daffodils might change colour. Most of what we know is *a posteriori* since it requires both an initial input from the senses and its continuing support. Knowledge of our friends, our world, our bodies comes via the senses. This knowledge changes all the time since the world changes all the time. Our senses have to be continually updated.

Types of Judgement: Analytic and Synthetic

The other Kantian terms, analytic and synthetic, do not refer to the way that you know a claim, but refer to the *meaning* of the claims themselves. Analytic judgements, says Kant, are where the 'predicate' is 'contained in the subject'.

'Predicate' and 'subject' are old and perhaps unfamiliar grammatical terms, but the idea is easy to grasp. If I say that a bachelor is an unmarried man, we can see that the ideas of unmarried and man are part of (contained in) the notion of a bachelor. The idea of a bachelor *is* the idea of an unmarried man. In other words, the predicate ('is an unmarried man') is contained in the idea of the subject (bachelor). We find that when we break down or analyze the claim, we have a kind of identity of concepts.

Synthetic claims, in contrast, are where the notion of the predicate is *not* contained in the notion of the subject. If I claim that bachelors are unhappy, then that is to add something extra to the idea of bachelor, which is not already contained in the notion itself. Again, if I say that trees require photosynthesis, I am finding out something about trees which is not just part of the meaning of the word 'tree'. It is a synthetic statement. Such a statement 'amplifies my knowledge by adding something to my concept' (1783).

Most of the claims we make are synthetic. This is because we are curious animals always seeking out genuinely *new* information, not just the unpacking of our words and terms. It is absurd to want to find out if bachelors are unmarried or not, but it is not absurd to want to find out if bachelors are happy or not. That is an extra bit of information which is not contained in the idea of a bachelor – it is an amplification or genuine expansion of knowledge.

Putting the Terms Together

The table below shows the combinations that we get if we combine these four terms:

Analytic Judgements	Synthetic Judgements
1) Analytic *a priori*	2) Synthetic *a priori*
3) Analytic *a posteriori*	4) Synthetic *a posteriori*

Analytic *a priori*

An analytic *a priori* claim is relatively straightforward. Here we have a claim where the judgement is really only an unpacking of what was already implicit in the subject. This is its analytic nature. But this must be known *a priori*. It is independent of experience since the judgement is not dependent upon experience. We do not have to wait and see if bachelors remain bachelors if they marry. A survey of known bachelors would be absurd if its first question was 'Are you unmarried?' If he is a bachelor he *must* be unmarried. It just follows from the terms used.

This implies that *all* analytic claims are *a priori*. You simply cannot have a case where there is an analytic claim, but where the judgement continues to be dependent upon experience. That means that box 3 must be left blank. There cannot be a claim which is analytic and also *a posteriori*. They simply don't work together.

Here are the types of claim which are left:

Analytic Judgements	Synthetic Judgements
1) Analytic *a priori*	2) Synthetic *a priori*
3) **Blank** <small>(There cannot be any analytic *a posteriori* judgements.)</small>	4) Synthetic *a posteriori*

Synthetic *a posteriori*

Synthetic *a posteriori* claims are also straightforward. In a synthetic judgement we have a claim where the judgement being made is *not* contained in the terms used. This seems to imply that we have to rely upon experience and continue to do so in order to know the claim – our example of bachelors being unhappy is known *a posteriori* (after experience). Updates are constantly required. After all, bachelors might find new ways to fulfil themselves even if they are at present unhappy about being single. This kind of knowledge is capable of changing. It is the same with our knowledge about trees needing photosynthesis. It is continually dependent upon experience. We might discover a new type of tree, perhaps some kind of cave-dwelling one, which does not require photosynthesis.

Most of the judgements we make are in the category of the synthetic *a posteriori*. We are on the continual look out for new information to amplify our knowledge. We do this by looking, testing, sensing, asking. We constantly make the attempt to attach new predicates to subjects. For example, we used to think that air was an element, but now we have discovered that it is not. It is a mixture of different gases. In the case of this kind of discovery, scientists were not unpacking the meaning of a word; they were not conducting an analytic investigation into the meaning of the words 'air' and 'element'. This kind of discovery is about finding out what *does not belong* to the meaning of a subject term, and so finding out extra and new information. We do this by using experience, and think we are justified by our experiments in attaching the new predicate 'is a mixture' to the subject term 'air'.

Synthetic *a priori*

We have one category left: the synthetic *a priori*, which is the most important category of judgement. For this type, we would have a judgement which is not continually reliant upon empirical or experiential methods (since it is *a priori*), but nevertheless, we would have new information which is not just an unpacking of terms and their meanings (since it is synthetic and not analytic). We would have amplification of knowledge without looking and seeing or any other kind of *a posteriori* investigation.

It seems, at first sight, that there cannot be such a judgement. Surely if we *discover* something about the world it must be done by *empirical* investigation such as looking and seeing, for example. The apparent impossibility of this judgement is why it is the most famous and the most controversial of the categories which Kant proposes, and, as we have seen, the main aim of the *Critique* is to answer the question of how such judgements are possible.

We can begin to get deeper into Kant's claim by looking at an example. Kant puts forward the following as a synthetic *a priori* judgement: 'All changes in the determinations (states) of substance take place in conformity with the law of the connection of cause and effect.' (1787)

What does this mean? Basically Kant is saying that all events must have a cause. This certainly does not look like an analytic claim. We do not appear to be merely unpacking the meaning of the word 'event'. If it is not analytic, however, it must be synthetic. Let us accept, then, that it is synthetic.

But that is not the most controversial part of the claim. Kant also claims that such a judgement is *a priori*. Here Kant is reacting to the great philosopher, David Hume, who had argued very convincingly that all judgements about cause and effect come from and depend upon experience. In other words, they are all inevitably *a posteriori*. In order to appreciate the nature of Kant's claims, we must briefly examine Hume's ideas about causation.

Hume on Cause and Effect

Hume argues in the *Enquiry Concerning Human Understanding* (1748) that without the input from experience, we would have no way of knowing what causally follows from what. (The book was translated into German in 1756, and there is good evidence that Kant read it, but we cannot be sure. He certainly knew *of* Hume's views from wider reading.) He gives some pretty convincing examples. Here is one. He asks us to imagine a superhuman with a super intellect who is looking at some water, but has had no experience of anything like water before. Would he, by just thinking about it, i.e., by *a priori* methods, be able to ascertain that the water is capable of drowning him? In other words, could even he, with superhuman powers of reasoning, be able *a priori* to understand that one of water's effects is to drown people who are immersed in it? Of course not, says Hume. He has to wait for information from experience. Only experience can inform him of that. Hume concludes from this and other arguments that we have to be *a posteriori* about cause and effect.

Hume went on to develop a highly psychological account of causation. He says that there are no real connections between events in the world (since such connections are not perceived by the senses and this method is for him the only way we can have knowledge about the world). All we really have are repetitions of the same kinds of pairs of events. Eventually when enough repetitions of cause and effect have happened, we are so mentally bludgeoned by the repeated pairs of instances that in the presence of one, we expect the other. Pick up a pen. Open your hand. What do you expect? You expect it to fall. This expectation, he says, is a kind of habit which finds its way into us by the sheer repetition of objects falling when hands have released them. Hume thinks of the relation of cause and effect as no more than a custom or habit of mind. It is merely a kind of psychological link.

This kind of account of causation worried Kant deeply. If there is no real causation, just habits built up from experience learned by only *a posteriori* methods, it threatens all of knowledge. Our world threatens to fall apart into unrelated sets of momentary disconnected instances rather than being an interconnected world with objective causes and effects.

So where does Hume go wrong? As far as Kant is concerned, Hume's mistake is to think that there are only two types of judgement – the *a priori* analytic and the *a posteriori* synthetic. Hume calls the first 'relations of ideas' and the second 'matters of fact'. But, as we have seen, Kant thinks there is a third option – the synthetic *a priori*, and the law 'all events have a cause' is, Kant thinks, one such example.

Why does Kant think it is *a priori*? He says that the law of cause and effect is not learned from experience. How could it be? First, we have not seen *all* causes and *all* effects, so how can the law be established if it is merely *a posteriori*? No, for Kant, the outside world does not just impose habits of thinking as if bludgeoning us from the outside. We are not just the passive servants of an exterior power. Kant's central insight is this: in experience we are as much *makers* of that experience as we are observers of it.

But what exactly does he mean by this? What Kant is saying is that we impose certain inevitable structures on experience as a pre-condition of it being an experience at all. Kant claims that the relation of cause and effect is an *a priori* structuring with which the mind makes sense of the raw material of experience. Without this structuring there would be no experience at all – just a booming, buzzing, nonsensical confusion or a 'rhapsody of sensation' as Kant calls it (1787).

We only really have an experience once it has passed through certain inevitable structuring filters. Cause and effect, for Kant, are part of this filtering process. They are, as it were, *a priori* moulds into which the raw material of the 'experience' is poured and the shapes it makes are inevitable. Experience simply wouldn't be experience unless it was moulded in this way.

Let us conduct the following thought experiment to appreciate something of what Kant means. Try to see everything you experience now as merely an unconnected series of momentary instances with one second having absolutely nothing to do with the previous one and nothing to do with the next. When reading this book, don't read these sentences as wholes (for that would be to connect your experiences into something like cause and effect), instead break them up into discontinuous atoms which exist as non-communal and entirely separate singularities. Tear apart and fragment the whole of your experience. If you can do this, experience falls apart and disintegrates. Sentences lose sense, and become meaningless noises. It isn't 'experience' anymore. In order for you to experience, you are automatically connecting all the time. It is as if you are imposing an order of cause and effect upon the whole way you experience the world.

Kant recalls the moment when he realized that experience itself is a structuring and unifying action. He likens it to the moment Copernicus shifted attention from the supposed movement of the sun to the movement of our own planet. In the Copernican revolution, Earth was no longer the stable centre of the universe that we had previously envisaged. Analogously, in the realm of human knowledge, we are not the passive receivers or copiers of impressions, as though mere passive satellites of experience (which was Hume's view), but the active planetary participators in the action of experience. Kant says,

> 'it has hitherto been assumed that all knowledge must conform to objects. [But this has proved a] failure. We must therefore make trial whether we may not have more success in the tasks of metaphysics if we suppose that objects must conform to our knowledge [...] We should then be proceeding precisely along those lines of Copernicus' principal thought.' (1787)

Copernicus shifted the way we perceived the universe from one point of view to another. And so, in metaphysics, Kant insists that instead of just supposing that objects impress themselves upon the experiencing subject, we must appreciate the contribution the experiencing subject makes to the raw materials of experience. The nature of the human knower is centre stage now. The perceiver must mould experience according to pre-given *a priori* conditions.

How is Synthetic *A Priori* Knowledge Possible?

Recall the distinction between analytic and synthetic judgements. Analytic judgements such as 'Bachelors are unmarried men' or 'Vixens are female foxes' are about the way that concepts work together. We find that certain concepts are joined to others in certain ways. One can be part of another, or even be identical to another. Kant says that in analytic judgements the predicate is contained in the subject. Note how this is now all about *concepts* – there does not seem to be much about empirical reality here, just how ideas relate to each other (which is why Hume calls these kinds of judgements 'relations of *ideas*').

In contrast, synthetic judgements like 'Air is a mixture' or 'Daffodils are yellow' are where we find we have to join a predicate to a subject. Such judgements seem to be genuinely informative about the nature of reality in a way that seems to be lacking in analytic claims. They add to our knowledge or amplify it.

This means that an *a priori* synthetic judgement would be one where we get information about reality, but can arrive at that judgement *before experience has told us about it*. This is, as we have seen, an amazing claim. Surely we have to wait until experience has given us information about what reality is like. But with Kant's Copernican revolution we can know beforehand what reality is going to be like by applying pure *a priori* reason.

Experience comes packaged by the experiencing subject because, in order to have any kind of experience, we must have done some *a priori* work upon the structureless deliveries of the senses. But, Kant reasons, if we can know what the *a priori* pre-packaging work is, we shall know what experience is going to be like before we have had it. We shall have *a priori* synthetic knowledge.

Recall the example of reading a book or a sentence. The words are connected into strings or meaning. You cannot have the experience unless it is connected. An unconnected series of utterly disparate momentary flashes (with no memory of the previous one) does not seem to be experience worth the name. If experience has to be packaged or connected together in some organizing matrix like cause and effect, we know, before any experience, that that is what it is going to be like. We shall know that it will be connected in some fashion.

We have thus far used the law of cause and effect to illustrate Kant's ideas. Let us now turn to two other forms of structuring that Kant thinks we impose upon the raw deliveries of the senses. This will help to further clarify what Kant means. Space and time are, according to Kant, both forms of inevitable structuring.

Space and Time: *A Priori* Structures of Experience

We automatically think of space as something we inhabit, as something that is outside us. Space, we tend to think, would be there even if there were no experiencing subjects. But according to Kant's radical view, space is a form of structural imposition – a kind of organizing matrix – which is necessary for experience to be enjoyed. In this understanding, we impose space upon the babble of sensory input in order that the babble is made to make sense. Only then can there be any experience at all.

Many scholars use an admittedly crude analogy to try to get this idea across. Space (and time), they say, are kinds of spectacles that we inevitably look through and consequently through which everything is experienced. Removal of the spectacles does not *blur* experience; it *removes* it all together. Space and time are inevitable 'colourings' which organize inputs so they can be filtered through to make experience for the observer.

This seems, at first, wildly implausible. How can the things that we see and hear be in a space that is of our own making? How can we walk about inside our own heads, which seems to be implied if space is created by the observer? Despite its strangeness, however, we do have science-fiction stories that demand a similar kind of understanding of space.

The film *The Matrix* (1999) is one such example. The main character Neo knows that there is something wrong with the world. He appears to walk around in an entirely real and normal American city. He seems to have a job, and to work at his entirely real and normal desk. However, he suspects that somehow things are not quite right. Eventually he discovers that an incredibly advanced AI system is feeding everyone an entirely illusory city landscape. The streets he walks, his job, the desk he sits at, are all ultimately not real. Even his own body is not real. They are digital inputs from the AI computer. In this science-fiction scenario, the space of the apparently external city is part of Neo himself. It is not outside him, but inside him. His mind surrounds the sky above and all the planets. He walks the streets in his own head.

Of course, this is only an analogy and has its limitations. For Kant, *all* space is a structural imposition upon the structureless chaos of sensory inputs. In the film we eventually find that there is a real space outside of Neo. He discovers the real exterior world in which he actually exists has been ravaged by a war between mankind and machines, and it is in this different (spatial) world that the awakened Neo eventually finds himself.

It seems inevitable that we must think of Neo and his body inhabiting some kind of space. But Kant would argue that space is an *a priori* structuring of experience. He would claim that our very inability to imagine a non-spatial world for Neo and his body provides evidence that space is a structural imposition that we, as experiencing subjects, use as a kind of organizing matrix. For example, it is possible to imagine that the house we live in does not exist and yet everything else seems to remain sturdily intact. We can imagine that the UK does not exist and, again, other things seem to carry on. But can we imagine that *space* itself is taken away while everything else is left intact?

No, this does not seem possible. Imagining that space is taken away appears to take everything with it. Kant notes however that the opposite does not hold. It seems possible to imagine *all* objects absent from the world while leaving space itself as a kind of waiting receptacle. Space is required for objects, but objects are not required for space. It seems impossible to imagine that space is absent, but nevertheless objects remain. Perhaps Kant is right, and this is evidence that space itself is an *a priori* structuring that allows us to have experiences at all.

Kant uses this idea of space in further ways, for example, to explain certain mathematical certainties we have, especially in the field of geometry. (He thinks all mathematical statements are synthetic *a priori*.) Why is it that we can know before experience that all triangles must have angles which add up to two right angles? It is because we already know that they must conform to the structural laws of space. We can know this *a priori* since we are looking at the underlying laws which are already contained in our own forms of inevitable structuring. For Kant, this explains the way that, before we have ever seen a real triangle, we can work out what structure it must have. The laws of geometry that we discover *a priori* are independent of experience since they underlie the possibility of having experience at all. (Non-Euclidean geometries had not been explored in Kant's time.)

Similar arguments seem to apply for the idea of time. Indeed, the arguments seem even stronger. All experience seems to be ordered in time. An experience utterly devoid of temporal duration – a mere instant – does not seem possible as an experience. Again, Kant argues that time is a kind of organizing matrix through which sensory inputs pass in order that consciousness can have experiences.

So are Space and Time Real?

It is tempting to think that Kant is arguing that space and time are not real, that somehow we have to pass beyond these imposed, artificial, psychological barriers, and see the world as it really is – a kind of non-spatial and non-temporal ultimate reality. But this is not what Kant is saying. Space and time are the ways in which experience itself is ordered – an empirical science of the non-temporal and the non-spatial is, therefore, impossible. We are no longer talking about the world if we do that. After all, what experiential access to such a spaceless, timeless realm would we have? None at all if space and time are required for experience.

We live, then, in the world of the spatial and the temporal. This is the real empirical world that science investigates. We must not think of space and time as mere illusions, although theoretically speaking, we have to admit in the last analysis, that they are not ultimately real (if we understand by 'ultimately real' whatever is completely outside and independent of us).

Kant here makes an important distinction. The world as we know it, the experiential and empirical world of space and time, is what he calls the *phenomenal* world. This is the world of inevitable 'appearances' since without those representations of reality there would be no experiential world at all.

However, there is, 'beyond' the empirical world, a *noumenal* world which is the world as it is 'in itself", but this world is not one that is accessible since it is absolutely beyond the reach of experience. Kant insists that the world of houses and people and plants and events and occurrences is the real, objective world. It is not an illusion or even a shared hallucination. We cannot, like Neo, wake up in the noumenal world since in such a world there could be no experiences. In such a world we would be entirely unconscious, and therefore there could be no waking up. Nevertheless in some sense this world of things-in-themselves must exist to explain the inputs that we have. There is a world 'out there' but direct perception is impossible since all perception is mediated by the frameworks of space and time.

We shall see in Chapter 4 that Kant will use this distinction between the phenomenal and the noumenal world to argue that people are not just chains in the causal history of the universe, but are radically free. All rational beings are 'ends in themselves'.

The Limits of Reason

Kant has established many things. He believes that he has shown that we can know something about the necessary structures of experiential reality or the phenomenal world. We can unite the *a priori* and the synthetic and have undeniable knowledge about the world when it comes to general over-arching structures. We can know that events will be in time, and objects will be in space. We can have confidence in the *a priori* synthetic conclusions of mathematics and geometry. Furthermore, we can know that experience must be connected up in regular, law-like ways. This is the positive message of the *Critique*. Have faith in reason – it can reveal the underlying structures of reality.

There is, however, a flip side to this. Kant also wants to warn us of letting metaphysics go beyond its proper boundaries. As we saw in Chapter 2, many philosophers were so confident in the power of human reason that they thought many other things could be put beyond rational doubt. For example, they thought that the existence of God could be proved and that the soul exists and could be proved to be immortal.

In the *Critique*, Kant argues that these kinds of belief cannot be established by pure reason. This is the criticism of pure reason suggested by the title of his work. Reason, when it is purely *a priori*, cannot go beyond its proper boundaries. When we do so we just end up with a 'battle-field of endless controversies' (1781).

This more critical side of Kant's work is expressed clearly in one of the most quoted parts of his works: 'Without sensibility no object would be given to us, without understanding no object would be thought. Thoughts without content are empty, intuitions without concepts are blind.' (1787) In other words, we need the input from the senses, but on its own this is not enough; we also need to conceptualize what we perceive as well. Thoughts needs objects to think about and this is given through the senses, but these objects are themselves filtered by the perceiver. They are conceptualized.

We have already seen this. The experiencing subject doesn't just experience as if information comes from the outside and is copied passively by its recipient. We *make* the experience as well by putting it under certain frameworks; overall frameworks like space and time are examples. But Kant thinks that this need for the dual work of sensory information and certain conceptual or structural impositions is applicable to all knowledge.

Putting it into Practice

Here is a simple, practical example. Look at whatever is in front of you. In order to make the experiment work, you must try to refrain from making any judgements about it. You must just allow the scene to make its impact, *but that is all*. Do not, for example, think to yourself 'There is a book' or 'There is my hand'. Refrain from any mental comment. Just allow the flurry of colours and shapes to make their impact without *thinking* of them as shapes and colours. That would be to make a judgement. Just perceive without judgement. Don't think of the objects as being in space or time – that also would be to make a judgement. Keep your senses receptive, but don't do anything with what you perceive. Is this possible? Can you just see without forming a judgement about what you see?

Of course it is immensely difficult. Perhaps it is impossible. The nearest we might come to it is when a person is coming round from unconsciousness and the scene makes an impact upon his or her sensory system, but they are not yet conscious enough to form a judgement. The only-just-conscious person will have just a bare picture without any content in terms of judgement like 'There's a pillow', or 'There's a window'.

Now we might ask, is this bare, non-judgemental experience enough to make knowledge? Of course not, because we *refrained* from making any kind of judgement upon it. We carefully stopped ourselves from forming a sentence about it. Only if you form some kind of judgement can knowledge come to be. It is thoughts akin to these that Kant believes show that sensory input on its own is not knowledge. It has to be added to something. In other words, the sense organs do not deliver knowledge although they might be essential to it. Philosophers would say that sense experience may be a necessity but it is not a sufficient condition for knowledge.

Let us try the experiment again, but this time do it the other way around. Let us try to make a judgement, but now remove any kind of sensory experience. Just judge without any experience. Don't picture anything. Keep your mind empty of sound, colour, taste, feel and smell. Again, this seems extremely difficult if not impossible. Even in a sensory deprivation tank a little bit of sensory input seeps through, and even if it didn't, you have a rich diet of past sensations and memories that keep coming to mind even if you try to block them out.

Probably the only way to achieve a bare, empty, experience-free desert would be to never have had any experiences at all, to have had every nerve ending severed so that the mind was kept closed and dark and blind. We might therefore conclude that without experience there does not seem enough to go on for us to form a judgement. (Note that, even to have formed the judgement 'My mind is empty', one must be acknowledging some kind of experience.) This seems to show, or at least suggest, that some kind of sensory input is needed to provide content for thought. Without it, 'thought is empty'.

Practical Reason

When talking about God or the soul, Kant thinks we simply do not have any idea what we are saying since there is no sensory information to work upon. Here we have 'thought without content' since there has been no sensory input. This sort of thinking is merely *speculative* metaphysics – a series of contentless ideas where we grope around in the dark: '[a lot] of metaphysics has hitherto been a random groping, and worst of all, a groping amongst mere [contentless] concepts' (1787).

As mentioned earlier, this scepticism concerning our ability to have knowledge about God, the soul and freedom of will is accompanied by Kant's insistence that beliefs about all these things are still legitimate. They just need to be slotted into their proper place. They are, he says, 'postulates of *practical* reason'. In other words, they are beliefs which are required by practical necessity. Kant says that we find we need to believe in these things in order to make overall sense of our lives since we are not just theoreticians. We live in worlds other than the purely scientific and mathematical. We live in a moral world as well. The next chapter will explore these issues.

4. The Categorical Imperative

Kant thinks we are not just *theoretical* reasoners; we also use *practical* reason. But what is the difference? As theoretical reasoners we are looking at the way things *are*. We are describing or theorizing about the world as it is. We have seen that Kant thinks we can go a long way in this – there are some general *a priori* synthetic frameworks which must apply to all experience – space, time and causality being three of these. As practical reasoners, on the other hand, we are not describing or exploring the way things are, but the ways things *ought* to be. We are seeking to change the world, and for this we need practical reason.

Kant does not think of practical reason as some kind of poor relation to theoretical reason. It is another crucially important part of our lives as rational beings. What ought to be the case is just as important (indeed Kant thinks more important) than what is the case. The way things ought to be is, of course, the domain of ethics or morality. It is inherently practical, and that is why Kant calls his second *Critique*, the *Critique of Practical Reason*. Kant wrote a more easily accessible account of his ethics called *The Groundwork* (sometimes translated as *Foundations*) *of the Metaphysics of Morals*. It was published before the second *Critique* and most students read *The Groundwork* first.

The Categorical Nature of Morality

The most important idea in Kantian ethics is the idea of duty, which is often called a *deontological* approach to ethics. We are duty bound to do certain things and to refrain from doing other things. In other words, we are under certain obligations. When these obligations are moral ones we can recognize that they are absolutely binding – they are, to use Kant's terminology, *categorical*.

Let's flesh this out by looking at a specific example of what Kant means by the absolutely binding or categorical nature of obligation or duty. We shall explore an example based upon a famous illustration that Kant himself gives in the *Metaphysics of Morals* – the example of the grocer.

Kant's grocer is an honest one. He gives the correct change even to those customers who he could easily fool. The honest grocer, perhaps in his heart of hearts, is sometimes tempted to give the incorrect change but he overcomes his inclination to make more money for himself, and always gives the correct change. Because of this we can call him an honest grocer.

Kant, however, invites us to delve a little further into the motives that this honest grocer might have. What reasons might the grocer have for giving the correct change? One set of thoughts might be like this: 'I could get away with giving the incorrect change, but it is also possible that one day I'll be found out. In that case, my reputation will be destroyed, and I'll lose customers. Because of this, I'd better give the correct change.' Is the grocer being truly moral in his honesty?

Kant invites us to recognize that if the grocer is acting out of these kinds of motive, then his actions are not really moral actions. Deep down he is thinking of himself and his own reputation.

He does not want to risk losing customers. Kant agrees that we would not go so far as to call the grocer *immoral* – after all, he is doing the right thing by always giving his customers the correct change. But Kant says that we recognize that the grocer's actions would be lacking in true moral worth if this was his motivation. Kant calls his motives *prudential*: honesty is to be preferred because dishonesty comes with a potential price tag of loss of reputation and a loss of trade.

We could look at this from a slightly different angle. If the grocer is acting out of these prudential motives, it is as if he is saying, 'If I could get away with it, I would be dishonest. But I cannot be absolutely sure that I will get away with it, so I'd better act honestly.' The grocer's honesty is here *highly dependent upon circumstances*. If things were different – if he could get away with dishonesty – it looks like he would cheat his customers. Is the grocer truly acting with any real moral worth? If we recognize that the grocer's actions are without moral worth, we must ask, says Kant, what kind of motives do count as truly moral?

Kant claims that the truly moral grocer is one who treats being honest as his duty. For this grocer, honesty is not just the best policy; it is the right thing to do. He regards dishonesty as simply immoral and so regards himself as duty bound to refrain from it.

Kant concludes that when someone does something out of a recognition that it is the right thing to do, then the act is truly moral. Doing the right thing for duty's sake is always good. Note that this kind of motive is *not dependent upon circumstances*: even if he could get away with it, our truly moral grocer would continue to do the right thing since he is doing it simply because he is responding to the call of duty. He is acting *categorically*.

The Good Will

When someone has motivations which are pure like the truly honest grocer, then we have what Kant calls a *good will*. In the *Metaphysics of Morals* he says the good will is the only thing in the world which is absolutely good: 'It is impossible to conceive anything in the world, or even out of it, which can be taken as good without qualification, except a good will.' (1785)

There are, Kant acknowledges, plenty of other good things. He lists quite a few: intelligence, wit, judgement. He calls these talents of the mind. There are also gifts of temperament like courage, resolution, constancy of purpose. Finally, there are also gifts of fortune or luck, like power, wealth, honour and health. All these things are obviously good, but are they *always* good? Are they good 'without qualification'?

No, says Kant. All these things can be turned to evil purposes. To use a non-Kantian example, the courage, intelligence and careful judgement of a dedicated serial killer are not good. It would be better for everyone if he were a coward and was insipid and inconstant. The important thing is not a gift of temperament, but how it is used. But what is it that determines how it is used? It is the *will* of the person. The will controls how you use temperaments. The will is either good or bad, and can turn good gifts into evil tools.

Kant concludes that the will, when motivated correctly, is the only thing that is good without qualification. Kant is well aware that some might object to this. 'What about *happiness?*' they would say. Is not this another unqualified value – one that is always good? Surely it is always good to be happy. Many philosophers of Kant's day certainly thought so, and many would agree today. But even happiness, Kant argues, is not good all the time. He writes,

> 'a rational and impartial spectator can never feel approval in contemplating the uninterrupted prosperity of a being graced by no touch of a pure and good will, and that consequently a good will seems to constitute the indispensable condition of our very worthiness to be happy.' (1785)

In other words, it is not good if a person who is evil is happy. Only those with a good will deserve such a peaceful and reposed state of mind. Imagine we found that the Commandant of the Bergen-Belsen concentration camp in Nazi Germany was blissfully happy and content with his murderous anti-Semitism. This would not be a good happiness. In fact, surely it would be a terrible and monstrously unjust happiness. No, justice demands that only those with a good will should have the bliss of happiness.

What it all comes down to is this: the part of us which determines our actions – the will – is the only thing that can be good without any qualification, and its goodness lies in its intention to do the right thing for its own sake. Everything else with a claim to being good flows from this source and depends upon this. The good will is the fount and determiner of goodness since it alone is under our pure control. Luck must play no part in the evaluation of moral action.

Two Types of Paralysis

Kant uses a couple of examples to force home his central point. Imagine that a person is extremely unlucky and is unable to accomplish anything. They entirely lack the power to act on their intentions. We might think of someone who is completely paralyzed, but conscious, for example.

Imagine, however, that they are trying by their utmost efforts to do the right thing. They strive mentally every day to do their duty, but cannot accomplish anything physically. For example, we might think of them earnestly wanting to help others in need on the hospital ward they share, but are unable to do anything to accomplish this. Now, asks Kant, would the lack of their being physically effective in this endeavour detract from their inner goodness? No, he insists, their good will would 'still shine like a jewel for its own sake as something which has its full value in itself' (1785).

Imagine another person. This time the person, through no fault of their own, entirely lacks the ability to empathize. They have not been lucky enough to be endowed with a temperament that finds enjoyment in doing good deeds. We might say that this person has a kind of emotional paralysis, rather than our former example of a physical paralysis. Can such a person still be good? Yes, insists Kant – a person who is motivated by duty, despite the emotional hardness of their temperament, has a 'moral worth and beyond all comparison the highest – namely that he does good, not from inclination [their temperament], but from duty' (1785).

Why is the moral worth of the hard-hearted beyond all compare if they have to strive to do the right thing? The answer is that people who do good deeds naturally are already inclined that way, and so they have a lucky temperamental advantage. For that reason, however, there is a danger. Are they doing good deeds because it makes them feel good? The answer often seems to be 'yes'. Kant says such people find an 'inner pleasure in spreading happiness around them and can take delight in the contentment of others' (1785). But this implies that they are not doing good deeds because it is their duty, but because they are getting an emotional reward. Now things are dangerously dependent upon circumstance.

There is no such danger, however, with the naturally hard-hearted. The emotional contentment of others leaves them emotionally untouched. Consequently, the hard-hearted can do good deeds wholly from a sense of duty since there is no other source of motivation. This is why their actions deserve so much moral praise.

Critics sometimes accuse Kant of being too cold here. Surely a person who naturally has sympathy with others and enjoys spreading happiness is a good person. After all, don't we want the hard-hearted to find joy in the doing of good deeds? Don't we want to be the kind of people who find joy and delight in helping others? Kant insists, however, that actions of this kind, when they are motivated by inner pleasure and delight 'however right and however amiable [they] may be', have no real moral worth (1785).

To understand Kant here, think of it this way. As we have seen, Kant says we must do the moral thing for the right reasons. We must do it because it is our duty. To do it for any other reason *makes it non-categorical.* Imagine the cheerful do-gooder is transformed overnight and becomes hard-hearted and emotionally cold. Now we have the real test of their goodness. Do they, despite now having no motivation of pleasure or delight, still continue to do the right thing? Do they still do sponsored runs and visit their elderly relatives? If not, we can suspect that they were really doing these things because it gave them pleasure.

Kant agrees that their pleasure in helping others is certainly attractive in a surface way, but it is not the deep down goodness which he is trying to identify – the noble, supreme, sacrificial goodness of someone who does good things purely for the sake of duty. This person is doing good deeds categorically without relying upon their temperament to provide the necessary motivation. These people are the true moral heroes. They are taking morality seriously enough to recognize its absolute call.

What and Where is my Duty?

Now Kant has to answer an important question: What exactly is it that we are required to do, or are prohibited from doing? We might agree that we must do the right thing for the sake of doing the right thing, but this is relatively uninformative unless we know what the right thing is. Indeed, we might ask: 'What if the person does awful things because they think it is their duty?' For example, some Nazis, when put on trial, gave a kind of Kantian excuse for their actions. They said they did not want to participate in atrocities, but forced themselves to do it because they thought it was their duty. Doing things for duty's sake is all well and good if we identify the right duties, but the Nazi example shows that following duty blindly is extremely dangerous. So how do we find out what our real duties are?

Kant has an answer, but to understand it, we must make a short digression. We must first look at *where* our duty is to be found. Only then can we know *what* our duty is. Kant reminds us that real, unqualified goodness lies in the will. Goodness does not arise from the *consequences* of our actions otherwise the paralyzed man cannot be good because so few consequences can flow from his frustrated intentions.

Moreover, it cannot be from our temperaments since then we might be doing good things just because we are temperamentally inclined that way, and not because we are treating the right things to do as categorical or absolute. Kant insists that the shining jewel of goodness lies deep within us, in the inner mental citadel where we decide what we are going to do.

This means that this seat of decision making – this inner part of us that decides what to do – must find the right principle of action *within itself.* We must find our duty not from looking outward, but looking inward. The will must find what to do from its own resources. Kant calls this *autonomy* – weighing the principle of action within ourselves, recognizing that it is our duty, and doing it. In other words, we have to legislate for ourselves; be our own moral judge. This is hard to understand, so let's look at what it does *not* mean, so we can narrow it down.

Imagine a person who obeys all the Ten Commandments. He has been taught that the Commandments are to be followed and is therefore convinced that they must be. Consequently he does not steal, he does not murder, he does not commit adultery and he is never envious. Many people might be tempted to think of this person as good, but as far as Kant is concerned this person is in danger of acting with the wrong source of motivation. Does he recognize his actions as right or is he just blindly following the Ten Commandments? If the latter, then what exactly is morally commendable about that? Doesn't this blind obedience to an external authority make his ethics dependent rather than categorical? After all, if the Ten Commandments had somehow been written wrongly and stated 'Do commit adultery', 'Do commit murder', and so on, would he robotically obey that instead? So the Kantian might ask: How does this person know that the Ten Commandments are the right commands to obey?

He must, of course, obey what he recognizes to be right, but he cannot recognize the legitimate authority of the Ten Commandments unless he has, beforehand, done some of his own moral thinking. Instead of blind unquestioning obedience to something outside himself, he must be *autonomous*. He must be the source of the moral law.

Kant is convinced that we have the resources within ourselves to be moral legislators since we are rational beings. We must pluck the correct principles of behaviour out of ourselves and then obey them simply because we recognize that the law thus produced is worthy of obedience. In Kant's grand conception, we should not be the blind, servile slave of an external authority, but the rational, practical thinker who is, through our own resources, uncovering and – in a sense – creating the moral code.

With this in mind, let us imagine a new, more enlightened follower of the Ten Commandments. She does not just blindly follow them, but examines them to see whether she agrees with them or not. She asks herself, what is so good about them? She must begin with her own judgement. (Of course, she might ask for the advice of others, but even here, she must judge herself whether the advice she is given is good.) The only real moral law, then, is one we must find for ourselves in the inner citadel of our own mind. The genuinely good will must submit to what it recognizes within itself as the correct kinds of behaviour.

Let us take stock. We have answered the question, '*Where* do we find our duty?' The answer is: within the inner citadel of the seat of decision making which is the will. But now we come to the crucial question, '*What* is the will to decide and *how*?' How are we to avoid everyone looking inward and coming up with their own bizarre and strange personal moralities? How are we to avoid someone thinking it is their duty to steal and lie? Kant believes that, if we use our minds correctly, then each rational being will find the same moral law since it is the inevitable outcome of thinking by each pure, practical will.

Let us give an example. It is the same one Kant gives in the *Metaphysics of Morals*, and concerns a false promise. Kant asks this question: 'May I not, when I am hard pressed, make a promise with the intention of not keeping it?' (1785). Imagine that at the deathbed of an elderly aunt, Tom promises that he shall give a proportion of his inheritance to charity. However, he secretly intends to keep the money for himself because he wants the money to pay off some debts. Should Tom do this? What is his duty?

Here the autonomous will immediately sets to work without relying on external authority. It tries to see what principles it should obey. Kant says Tom must decide what kind of action he is doing here. What is the rule Tom is following in this situation? Kant calls the rule or principle a person is following the maxim. The maxim or rule Tom is following is something like this: the rational will can intend to make a false promise.

Now Kant asks, is this the kind of action that can be consistently willed by the rational, practical will? Kant's answer is a firm, unequivocal no. It cannot be endorsed as a method of acting since it is rationally inconsistent. Tom, and any other practical reasoner, must realize that if they act in this way then they are, at the same time, recommending it as a principle of action for *all other rational wills*.

We might ask, 'Why is a kind of behaviour a recommendation for all others? Why can't I say it is just my personal choice?' The answer is that, if you do something but say that someone else cannot, you have to have a reason why. There must be a relevant difference between you. But as pure, rational wills we are all *exactly the same*. Remember there is no temperament in the will. The will rises above the temperaments and can make them good or bad by its decisions. Consequently there are no personal gifts to distinguish you. There is nothing but the source of decision making, and so, in this respect, each person is identical. It follows then that, when you do anything, you are implicitly *universalizing* it for all other wills. This means that moral choices are never personal choices, they are choices we make for a will that is identical to all other pure, rational wills.

As soon as we realize that, we must also realize that the maxim behind lying is inconsistent. Imagine that the rule 'Everyone must lie' was a principle that everyone had to follow. What would a world of universally prescribed lying be like? Kant points out that, in such a world, there could be no lying since everyone would know that the opposite of what you said was the truth. As Kant puts it, 'my maxim, as soon as it was made into a universal law, would be bound to annul itself' (1785).

Kant formulates a kind of test for maxims that the rational, practical will can use in its endeavours to find its duties. He calls it the 'categorical imperative': 'Act always such that the maxim of your action can at the same time be a universal law.' (1785)

If we are to possess a good will, we must obey the results that we discover as we explore the practical rationality of what we propose to do. To obey this inner law is to do our duty and that is always a good thing, and any will whose source of motivation is this inner law is like a shining jewel of goodness. We can see here Rousseau's influence on Kant that we explored in Chapter 2. For Rousseau, the general will is one that expresses what you actually legislate for yourself. It is through obedience to this inner law, which is one with the more general will, that you find you can free yourself from the bondage of desire. The universal will is identical with the pure, inner will.

Rational Beings as Ends-in-themselves

Kant has other ways in which he tries to express the moral law we discover and create by our own reasoning powers. We have just examined what is called the *First Formulation of the Categorical Imperative* – the initial way that Kant expresses the idea of a will trying to make sense of actions. For obvious reasons, it is often called the universalizability formulation. But he has other ways of expressing the categorical imperative.

Let us look at the second formulation (there are two more, but we won't examine them as it would take us too far afield). In many ways the second formulation is more obvious than the first, which can appear rather abstract and dry. The second formulation contains a kind of summary about the nature of the rational wills that are the centre of our moral lives:

> *'Act so that you treat humanity, whether in your own person or in the person of any other, always as an end, and never as a means only.'* (1785)

Kant says that humanity – and here he means any rational being – is an *end-in-itself*, and must be treated as such and never merely as a means. This implies that when I am proposing a maxim I must ask myself, 'Does the policy I am proposing merely use other people or does it respect them as precious in themselves? Is my behaviour towards other people the kind that merely uses them?' (For obvious reasons, this is often called the *humanity formulation*.)

Let us return to the example of Tom. Can Tom promise his aunt, but at the same time intend to break the promise? We saw how the first formulation showed the practical absurdity of this kind of action – the maxim annulled itself. How can the second formulation show that it is absurd? If Tom lies to his aunt, is he merely using her or is he respecting her? What is Tom's attitude towards his aunt when he proposes to falsely promise to give some of her money away to charity? It seems obvious that he is not respecting his aunt here since he is treating her as undeserving of the truth. We can see that, in his false promise, he shows that he regards the aunt as a mere means. He wants money, and his aunt is the means to get it. In other words, he is using his aunt instrumentally, rather than as a genuine rational being with an autonomous will of her own.

The idea behind the second formulation has become very influential in our moral thinking. For example, it provides an answer to the question, 'Why is slavery wrong?' The second formulation seems to answer this in an intuitive and plausible way: in slavery people become mere commodities. They are bought and sold. We are treating members of humanity solely as means to ends.

Note, by the way, that Kant does not think use of people is necessarily wrong in every circumstance. It is clear that we often have to use people such as when we employ people to do certain jobs. Are they being used as instruments or tools to get things done? Yes, they are being used, but that is acceptable as long as they are not being wholly treated as instruments or as 'means only'. In other words, we have to be careful how we treat people when we use them instrumentally.

What Exactly is an End-in-itself?

We have seen that the second formulation of the categorical imperative requires us to consider whether rational individuals are being (merely) used. We have summarized this as the idea that people are precious in themselves, or innately valuable, and because of this, they are not to be treated as mere tools. This is all true but there lies a deeper and more profound truth behind Kant's notion that rational beings are ends-in-themselves. We shall briefly explore this. It is an amazing account of our humanity.

In the last chapter we distinguished the difference between the phenomenal world and the noumenal world. The phenomenal world is the world as it appears to us as experiencing subjects. It comes packaged according to certain frameworks. This world is not an illusion, but the world in which we live out our lives. The noumenal world, on the other hand, is the world as it is in itself. Kant thinks that the noumenal world cannot be known, since it cannot be experienced. It is there, presumably not in space and time since both are aspects of our synthesising matrix, but still existent in some sense.

As living participators in the phenomenal world of experience, we order experience, seeking to unify it by applying causal laws: we see a window break – we seek a cause – it seems to be a stone that broke the glass. We unify events into groups. (Remember, when we try to atomize experience it falls apart.) This application of causal frameworks to the phenomenal world also applies to humanity itself since we too are part of that world. In the empirical world of science, Kant says that we humans have to see ourselves and our bodies as part of this causal network of cause and effect.

Scientists, for example, seek out the causes of behaviour. Neurophysiology treats people as extremely complicated causal, but essentially mechanistic, systems. A part of the brain is enlivened and a decision is made. It is connected by cause and effect. (Think of the current vogue of using MMR brain scans to try to show what a person is like. Here we think of parts of the brain causing people to be the kind of person they are.) On a *theoretical* level, Kant has no problem with the application of causality to human beings. It is a necessary part of the empirical pursuit in the world of phenomena.

But, on a practical level, what has made theoretical sense makes sense no longer. We have seen that Kant thinks that, as rational beings, we can follow the call of duty. We can test our maxims and see if they are practically incoherent, and the will can then decide to revere the moral law, rather than follow inclinations and desires. However, if we are just elaborate and complicated causal networks, then this seems impossible. Surely, if we are just cause and effect, won't we be *caused* to act according to whatever is the strongest desire? We won't be able to arbitrate between the different desires. We won't be in charge; we will just be the causal product of our past history.

Let us go back to the honest grocer to understand this vitally important point. The merely prudential grocer might well have been tempted to dupe his customers, but the desire for preserving his reputation overcame the temptation and so he gave the correct change. Here one desire overcame another and the strongest desire made the grocer hand over the correct change. This is essentially a cause and effect picture of human psychology. (It is one that Hume had endorsed and argued for.) The strongest desire is the one that we follow. Such a view is extremely popular today.

But if this is the entire truth it makes nonsense of Kant's picture. In his view, we are able to 'transcend' our desires; we can use our practical reason to see that some desires and their accompanying maxims are absurd, and we can *choose* not to go that way. This is not because we have another desire, but because reason tells us some desires are inconsistent. We *obey* the call of reason. We are not *caused* to behave by reason. We have a choice.

If we choose to go with our inclinations we are deciding to be the kind of being who just follows his appetites, and allows whatever is the strongest desire at that moment to hold sway. We are, in effect, deciding to be merely causal beings. This is presumably how an animal behaves. It does not choose the correct moral path, it just goes where its desires lead it. But reason allows a different path. In Kant's picture, we can be 'above the fray' so to speak, looking down on the action, and can decide what to do using our rational natures.

Kant admits that he cannot use pure reason to prove that we have this kind of radical freedom to choose and adjudicate between desires. On a theoretical level we inevitably seek causal law and understand ourselves to be causal beings, and on that level, Hume seems to be right. One desire will overcome another and we do that thing rather than this thing. We are slaves to desires and appetite. This seems to be the inevitable account that *theoretical* reason leads us towards.

But on another level, the practical level which Kant believes is more important, we cannot assume this is always true. We have to see ourselves as free beings – as beings who are genuinely responsible for our actions. Therefore we have to assume we are beings who transcend the causal nexus. In this picture, we have one foot in this phenomenal world of cause and effect and space and time, but we have to assume that we have the other foot in the noumenal world and we are able to escape the straitjackets of desire. We can rise above the phenomenal. We are, says Kant, in touch with the super-sensible, the arena of the ultimately real beyond space and time.

This is the principal reason that Kant calls us *ends-in-ourselves*. We can conclude, as part of practical reason, that *we are not just passive links in the causal chain*. When it is a rational person we have to assume that 'the buck stops here'. We are the first movers when we make decisions based upon the rational deliberations of the will. For Kant, this ability to be 'above' the physical world is what gives each one of us an incomparable dignity. A person is not merely a blind part of the causal process (like the stone that broke the window). Each person is an end-in-themself and as such is supremely dignified and possesses an invaluable inner worth.

Kant has a name for beliefs that are practically necessary, but are beyond the comprehension of the empirical self. They are called 'postulates of practical reason'. (He includes belief in God, freedom of the will and the immortality of the soul.) Only if we believe in such things will we be able to make overall sense of our lives.

Let us give a brief example. Our legal system seems to assume that we possess this kind of Kantian 'buck stops here' freedom. As long as people are not insane, we think that rational, adult people are, in at least some cases, the ultimate originators of what they do. They are ends-in-themselves. That is why we think people can be genuinely guilty. We cannot always blame the circumstances we find ourselves in. The guilt resides in us, not in the vicissitudes of the mechanistic, physical world.

If we did not think this, then we have to admit that no one is ultimately responsible for what they do. In this causal picture of human psychology, inputs go in, interact with the desire system, and the strongest desire causes the body to respond. We do good deeds or we do evil but it is not *chosen* – rather it is *caused*. In this conception, we cannot really obey the moral law; rather we are merely pulled hither and thither by the strongest impulsion. If we really believe that this is what we are, we cannot have the dignity that Kant thinks we possess. We are just elaborate mechanisms. We are helpless rag dolls in the jaws of desire.

So, to summarize the ideas of this section, Kant is saying that if morality is not an illusion, then we must suppose that we are radically free in the sense given. We are in ultimate control. We have the dignity of being morally responsible. In this way, it is a postulate of practical reason that we can rise above the compulsions and cravings of desire and become faithful followers of the moral law — a law that is discovered from within as we think through the logic of our actions.

5. What is Beauty?

Kant considered his last *Critique*, the *Critique of Judgement*, to be the bringing together or unification of his most important thoughts. It is a controversial work, not this time because of the complexity of the ideas contained within it (although there is plenty of that), but because critics are divided over whether it really is a work of genius or a baffling and poorly thought out mess – perhaps, some scholars speculate, a sign of Kant's failing mental health. Despite these negative assessments, many of the philosophers and artists who came immediately after Kant agreed with him and thought the work to be the crowning culmination of his genius. It contains some of the most influential ideas in the history of the philosophy of beauty or, as it came to be known in Kant's day, *aesthetics*.

To begin with, let us consider the following kinds of judgements about beauty that people might make about a particularly beautiful species of rose:

1. This rose is beautiful because it is the result of my many years of genetic research.

2. This rose is beautiful because it is going to make me a lot of money.

3. I find this rose beautiful because it reminds me of the happy years of my marriage.

4. I find this rose beautiful because it attracts a particularly rare kind of bee and has thus saved it from the brink of extinction.

5. This rose must inspire anyone with a sense of delight. It is something about the shape and the intricacy of its petals. There is an inexplicable fittingness or organization in the whole thing.

Kant would say that only the last of these statements is a judgement about beauty. The others are really about something else entirely. True judgements about beauty have, says Kant, four complementary aspects. He calls these aspects 'moments'. This can be misleading for the modern reader, but he means it in a technical sense borrowed from the physics of his day. We will also use the word 'moment', since it is the one used almost exclusively in the literature, but these four moments must be thought of as four mutually supporting and inseparable ways of understanding judgements about beauty. Only when all four have been explained can we see how they all fit together and appreciate each one.

Moment One: Disinterested Involvement

This is how Kant expresses this aspect of beauty:

> [True] Taste is the faculty of judging an object or a mode of representation by means of a delight or aversion apart from any interest. The object of such a delight is called beautiful. (1790)

Here Kant is following a line of thought that had been around for many years. He agreed with many others who said that, in order for a judgement to really be about beauty, it must be untainted by any interest. In other words, contemplation of beauty must be *disinterested* delight.

The word 'interest' here is being used in the sense where you have a stake in something. For example, someone is an *interested* party in the reading of a will if they stand to gain or lose something from the inheritance. We hope the presiding solicitor, however, is *dis*interested – a kind of neutral but involved arbiter able to make the right decisions since she has no stake in the outcome.

Many of the judgements that were listed earlier which attempted to concern beauty were really tainted by interest. Look back at the second judgement; there the person found the rose beautiful because they were going to make a lot of money. Here the person was not really focusing on the rose, but on the way that it was going to be a kind of tool to get from A to B: from poverty to wealth. The person had a monetary interest in the rose, rather than focusing on the beauty of the rose. They may have experienced delight, but it was not a disinterested delight.

This connects with the idea of an end-in-itself which we examined in Chapter 4. Judgements about beauty must not have an eye on the instrumental value of the beautiful object. If your eye is on the worth of the beautiful painting, then you are not really appreciating the beauty of the painting. The beauty is a kind of end-in-itself.

The first person sees the rose as the culmination of her efforts, the result of years of dedicated research. Her feelings are more about pride than they are about the rose's beauty. Again, the person who claims to find the rose beautiful because it reminds him of happier days is also inappropriately interested. He is not appreciating the beauty of the rose, but using it to get to his memories. Similarly, the bee saviour's appreciation of the rose is not an aesthetic delight, but a relief that the unfortunate bees are, at last, safe.

Obviously the motives that these three people have are more laudable than the one that is merely concerned with money. Nevertheless, according to Kant, they aren't really appreciating the beauty. To see beauty as having a purpose is to instrumentalize that which should be regarded as simply valuable in itself.

Kant explains this further by distinguishing appreciation of beauty from desire for what he calls the 'agreeable'. Some things, he notes, merely satisfy our appetites or the senses. For example, eating a hearty meal when hungry is delightful, but it is not a delight in the beautiful. Here the appetites are gratified. Moreover, you are an interested, not a disinterested party when you're hungry and a meal is offered. In order to truly appreciate something as beautiful you need to distance yourself from mere gratification. Indeed, Kant says if we want to find people with the finest, most well-developed tastes we have to seek out those whose needs have already been satisfied. Only then can the finest judgements be found.

Kant has another way of understanding this aspect of judgements concerning the beautiful. Judgements about beauty involve *contemplation*. You gaze and dwell upon the beautiful object with a sense of wonder. There is more than a glance, there is careful consideration. However, as soon as you want to possess it or use it, the beauty is obscured by another kind of judgement altogether. For example, imagine seeing a picture of some apples, thinking to yourself, 'How beautiful! They look so life-like and tasty that I wish they were real so I could eat one!' Is this response truly an appreciation of the beauty of the picture? No, says Kant, here you see the apples as agreeable to the senses and so you want to possess the apples. You have lost sight of the delightful contemplation of the picture.

This neutrality about a beautiful object's actual existence goes some way to explain how we are able to find fictional objects beautiful. Venus, the goddess of love, does not actually exist but we can find her beautiful, nevertheless. However, as soon as anyone desires this beautiful woman and wants her to actually exist, they betray their disinterested delight and submit to their appetites. Appreciation of beauty has turned to desire for gratification.

Moment Two: Universal Pleasure Without a Concept

Kant expresses this aspect of judgements about beauty as follows: 'The *beautiful* is that which, apart from a concept, pleases universally.' (1790) As can be seen, there are two parts to this moment. We will take the second part first. What does Kant mean by 'pleases universally'? He means that when something is appreciated as beautiful we make a claim that we think extends beyond our own immediate pleasure. We think, indeed we demand, that others too must find this beautiful. The judgement we make is meant to be one which extends to all other, right thinking, disinterested parties.

Examples of Universality

Here is an example. You climb a peak in the Lake District and stop to admire the view. There is a glistening lake at the bottom surrounded by gently undulating hills with a snaking, distant river leading to a cluster of old stone cottages. You declare it to be beautiful (without, of course, desiring it for yourself or thinking about the cottages' retail value on the property market!). You surely think others would come to the same conclusion. Imagine you have a friend that looks at the same prospect you admire and he says that it leaves him totally unmoved. You would be shocked, perhaps thinking to yourself that he was not in his right mind. You would think that something was getting in the way of his proper appreciation and delight.

This universality demanded in proper judgements about the beautiful is different from judgements about what merely gratifies us. For example, we do not mind if others find certain foods unappetizing. John might like the taste of hot chillies while Bob thinks they are disgusting. This is about the 'agreeable' in the sense outlined before. In these kinds of cases we do not demand that others agree with our tastes. Kant says:

> *As regards the agreeable everyone concedes that his judgement which he bases on private feeling, and in which he declares that an object pleases him, is restricted to himself personally. Thus he does not take it amiss, if when he says that Canary-wine is agreeable, another corrects the expression and reminds him that he ought to say: It is agreeable to me [...] A violet colour is to one soft and lovely, but to another dull and faded. One person likes the tone of wind instruments, another prefers that of string instruments.'* (1790)

Here is another difference between beauty and the agreeable. With the agreeable, we do not mind too much if others disagree with us. But we reserve a special status for judgements about beauty – we demand that there is consensus. Kant says that one who claims that something is beautiful 'demands this agreement from [others]. He blames them if they judge differently, and denies them taste, which he still requires of them as something they ought to have' (1790). So then, there is a universal claim in judgements about beauty that is not demanded when we find something merely gratifying or agreeable.

This connects with what we looked at in the last section – the idea that proper aesthetic delight is disinterested. When you are disinterested you are leaving your personal feelings behind. You separate yourself from the unique characteristics that make you different to others and are left with only the disinterested delight. It is therefore inevitable, says Kant, that the judgement is seen as demanding that others agree. You've left your personality out of the equation. Others who leave their personalities at the door in the contemplation of the beautiful will surely come to the same conclusion.

Think back to the unappreciative person who climbs the same peak you do and says that the beautiful prospect leaves him totally unmoved. It is unlikely that you think, 'Well then, it is just a beautiful prospect for *me*'. Because your delight is disinterested and not therefore dependent upon your personality you immediately think there is something wrong with your companion. He is surely allowing something personal in his life to get in the way. Kant says that you have to think this if your judgement is truly disinterested and not the result of your personal appetites.

There is then a universalizing demand in claims about the beautiful that is absent in that which we find agreeable due to our personal characteristics. Let us go onto the second part of this aspect of the beautiful – the idea that the beautiful is that which delights without concepts.

Understanding the 'Good'

To understand this claim, we have to first explore another kind of judgement that we might make about an object. We might, for example, call something good. Now Kant is convinced that the good and beautiful, although related, are different from each other. Claims about beauty are not the same as judgements which claim that something is good. Why is this? Kant says that when we say that 'X is good' there is always an implicit or underlying claim that it is *good for something*. For example, an expert sushi chef might call his incredibly sharp, sushi-knife 'good'. What he means by this is that it is excellent for creating very precise and delicate slices of raw fish. It is good at a particular purpose.

Imagine the chef lost the knife. He would want it back since he wants it to achieve the purpose for which it was designed. A purely fictional knife is not enough because an imaginary knife cannot cut fish. Judgements about the good imply an interest rather than the disinterest that Kant is concerned with.

To show this, let us imagine that instead of a sushi chef we have a collector of knives who is concerned wholly with beauty. Her appreciation is separated from personal interests like getting a job done. She loves the curve of the blade, the delicate thinness of the cutting edge. Of course, it would be hard to entirely divorce her appreciation of its usefulness from her appreciation of its beauty, but Kant insists they are separate judgements. Ideally the collector of knives, if she is wholly disinterested, would be content with a virtual knife – one that could be appreciated in some incredibly sophisticated virtual reality scenario. (We assume that this program allows her to feel the delicate weight and balance of the knife.) Here it could be appreciated as just beautiful – not good, of course, since a virtual knife cannot cut real fish.

Imagine that the collector was not content with the virtual beauty. What could be the reason for that? To Kant it would immediately imply that she wants the knife for something – it is no longer the disinterested contemplation of the beautiful. It might have turned into the agreeable, or it may have turned into a judgement about the good. Perhaps she wants to use the knife since it does its job so well. If this is so, then she has lost sight of the beautiful.

Kant gives an example which has become famous. He tries to make clear what he means by beauty being without a concept:

> '*To deem something good, I must always know what sort of a thing that object is intended to be, i.e. I must have a concept of it. That is not necessary to enable me to see the beauty in something. Flowers, free patterns, lines aimlessly intertwining – technically termed foliage – have no signification, depend upon no determinate concept, and yet please.*' (1790)

Consider one of the examples of false judgements that we explored at the beginning of this chapter. We can now understand that the person who claimed to see the flower as beautiful since it was excellent at attracting bees had actually conceptualized the rose. He saw it 'under a concept'. This means that the person instrumentalized the flower. He saw it as a good, rather than beautiful flower. A virtual one would not have satisfied such a person. He wants a real flower.

Let us contrast these kinds of responses with the final person – the response that Kant would have endorsed. Remember what she said:

> 5. This rose must inspire anyone with a sense of delight. It is, something about its shape and the intricacy of its petals. There is an inexplicable fittingness or organization in the whole thing.

This person sees the rose as beautiful. She is not able to say precisely why it is so pleasing. She is not trying to conceptualize the rose, but appreciates it wholly for the way that the shape of the petals cluster together. She does not want to possess the rose, nor make money from it. She does not want to see how good it is at some purpose. For her, a virtual flower would give her as much aesthetic delight as a real one.

We can note, also, that the final person thought others would surely share the appreciation of the beauty. She found herself automatically universalizing her response rather than merely thinking that it looked beautiful to her. Because her response was disinterested, it could be cool and detached, and not based upon any personal quirks or idiosyncrasies that she might have. She therefore sees no barrier that can come between other similarly disinterested people and the rose's beauty.

Universal Subjectivity

We have seen that part of the analysis of beauty that Kant offers is that judgements about beauty come with a kind of universalizing demand. We don't think such judgements are personal or idiosyncratic but that everyone in their right mind will come to the same kind of decision. From this it might be presumed that beauty is a kind of property that some things possess. That, after all, would explain the demand for universalization. If, for example, I judge that a box has the property 'square', I demand that others come to the same decision, and think there's something not right if they claim to see a triangle. Is beauty a property like 'square' then?

Many of Kant's contemporaries offered analyses of beauty like this. They tried to say what properties beauty actually boiled down to. Their thoughts were along the following lines: 'What properties do beautiful things share that will give us the properties that beauty actually depends upon? If we can answer this, we shall have found the secret springs of beauty!' One popular answer (based upon Aristotle) was that beauty is really a kind of balance, proportion or symmetry. When we say something is beautiful we are really declaring that it has these properties in some way. Kant calls these kinds of properties *objective* or empirical properties. They are the properties that are actually possessed by objects. As we have seen, if beauty is like this, it would explain why we think that others must agree with our judgements about beauty.

But Kant is adamant that his contemporaries were all wrong. Beauty, for Kant, is *subjective*. That is, it is reliant on feelings. When we say that something is beautiful it is not conceptual knowledge that we are attempting to communicate. Beauty is not a property that is in the rose. Judgements about beauty are dependent upon pleasure, and feeling pleasure is a subjective mental occurrence. For Kant, 'beauty is for itself, apart from any feeling of the subject, nothing'. (1790)

We think of the shape as something that is objectively there, independent of any pleasure that we might derive from it, but the beauty, says Kant, is not there in that manner. We would not know that beauty was present but for the pleasure. Indeed, Kant says that purely rational beings without any faculty for feeling pleasure would not report that things were beautiful. Our declarations about beauty would leave them mystified. To them, the Lake District view would presumably be a set of shapes laid out in a particular geometric configuration. They do, of course, see *exactly* what we see but they feel no pleasure. We do feel pleasure and so we say of such a scene, 'That is beautiful'. Furthermore, we demand and expect that others feel the same way.

Kant's rejection of beauty as a kind of objective property is, of course, due to his view that judgements about beauty are without concepts. If beauty were an objective property of the rose in the same way that the shape or symmetry is an objective property of the rose we would be able to conceptualize beauty – after all, we can do it with other objective properties like shape and size.

Furthermore, if claims about beauty were objective, then we could reason with people like our philistine of the Lake District. The one who appreciated the beauty would be able, using concepts and rules, to *prove* to the philistine that his aesthetic taste had erred. It would be like showing someone who thought he saw a triangle that it was really a square. But disagreements about beauty are very common, and if someone does not feel the universalizing pleasure that we ourselves experience, there seems to be no way that we can *show* him or her that they are wrong. Nonetheless, despite all this subjectivity, we remain disappointed with people who look upon Lake District views and are unmoved.

But how can that be? How can anyone demand that the judgement about the beauty of the rose be universalized if there is no property 'beauty' that the object possesses? If the pleasure arising from the contemplation of the rose is based upon feelings and not upon concepts, how can you justify your demand that this internal pleasure be universalized? Surely judgements about beauty are personal to you if they are merely subjective. Surely we should see the beautiful in the same way we see the agreeable or gratifying – a personal preference that is illegitimate to universalize.

We can put the problem slightly differently. Beauty is without concepts: it is based upon an immediate feeling when you see certain objects. This does not mean that beauty is private and incommunicable because when you say that the rose is beautiful, the claim is one that is about *the rose*, not your personal feelings. But this seems to imply that you are saying something objective about the rose. So claims about beauty seem both with and without concepts. How can we resolve this problem?

This question is answered in the next moment that Kant identifies as part of the four moments that he discusses. He says that the justification for the universalizing demand is in what he calls the 'purposiveness without a purpose' that you represent to yourself when responding to what you judge to be a beautiful object. We turn to that now.

Moment Three: Purposiveness Without Purpose

Kant defines this aspect of beauty as follows: '*Beauty* is a form of purposiveness in an object, so far as this is perceived in it *apart from the representation of an end*.' (1790) Kant spends a lot of time on this part of his analysis of beauty – the idea that, in the appreciation of beauty, there is a sense of a purpose without attributing an end or purpose. In other words, we see a kind of purpose but do not ask, 'What is it for?' His discussion is very complicated, but we can get to the essence of what he says by thinking clearly about the experience of a beautiful object.

Examples of Purposiveness

Think about the beauty of a rose. What is it you see? What is it you experience? The petals are a pattern of shapes related to each other in a certain way. They have a kind of structure or composition. Kant says that your mind represents it as a kind of organizational whole, which is close enough to what Kant means by the notion of purposiveness: we see some things as if they were organized without committing ourselves to what the organization is there for. This organization prompts a response of delight.

Let's try to make that clearer. Kant uses the example of coming upon a circular plot of grass in a forest. You think it is beautiful. The pattern of the trees and their size in relation to the plot seems to have a certain pleasing organization. You might speculate about this purposiveness a little more and try to find the purpose or end behind it. Perhaps, you think, it is used for country dances. Here you represent an end or purpose. Now, thinks Kant, the judgement about beauty is being replaced or, at least, sidelined. You were not content with its 'just rightness' or organization, but tried to go beyond that and questioned why it is there and what purpose it serves. The free appreciation you have has now been interrupted. You might think that the plot is too small, or too big, or just right, but even here the 'just right' would be about purpose, not about the beauty. (It would then have changed into a *good* plot.)

Another example Kant gives is of the expert botanist. She knows the true nature of the flower. She knows why it is there, why it is shaped like that. She knows the function of all the parts.

Her appreciation is about purposes and how good the plant is at what it does. Now think of the natural, uncluttered delight of a non-botanist. She does not think of the function of the parts, the ends to which each part is directed. Instead, there is freedom to wonder and contemplate. The free beauty of the flower is not functionalized. Flowers considered as such have 'no intrinsic meaning; they represent nothing – no object under a determinate concept – and are free beauties' (1790).

To Summarize

Beauty is subjective, because without the capacity for feeling pleasure, it is 'nothing'. Beings that are purely rational, with no capacity for feeling, see what we see but do not think of beauty. The beauty of a rose cannot be seen as an objective property that the rose possesses. Furthermore, we say things are beautiful if they strike us as organized (purposive) in certain ways, but we must not look beyond this and ask what the object is for. If we do, then the experience is conceptualized and the beautiful has to give way to the good.

For Kant purposiveness is the *structure* of the object – the pattern in the carpet, the complicated tracing of lines and shapes in a painting. It is the aimless intertwining of the lines upon a leaf. It is the pattern of movements in a dance or a piece of music. These are all things that are laid out in space and time. It is often simply called the *form*, which is the word that Kant uses to name the organizational structure of an object.

Kant has a particular reason why he concentrates so much on form or spatio-temporal structure. Remember, he wants justifying grounds for the universalization of judgements about beautiful objects. He does not want judgements about the beautiful to be on a par with judgements about the taste of chillies or wine. That is mere sensation. But surely *structures* like the pattern of hills and lakes in the Lake District is a perception that we all share. After all, everyone sees the same pattern. Structures seem more real and robust than tastes and smells. Why is that?

Spatio-temporal Structures

Recall that Kant, in the first *Critique* (Chapter 3), identifies space and time as being inevitable matrices that we impose in order to transform raw sensory inputs into experience. Space and time are among the most basic *a priori* intuitions. They are fundamental to experience. That is why Kant thinks that it must be the spatio-temporal structure or organization which is the basis for the universalizing pleasure that reports about beauty have. If judgements about beauty are not going to be merely individual personal judgements then we must have an *a priori* foundation in experience that is common to everyone and, for Kant, spatio-temporal structure can provide this stable universal basis.

For example, as we have seen (in the section Examples of Universality), Kant (perhaps surprisingly) rejects the notion that a particular colour can be beautiful. His reason is that colour is a mere sensation: how colour strikes the senses is too changeable from person to person. However, if we are talking about pattern and structure, we have something that is much more substantial and shareable. (Kant's theories led to a movement in art criticism called *Formalism*, and eventually to abstract painting which tried to use structure and pattern rather than representation.)

Kant is insistent then that beauty is subjective in the sense that it does not refer to any objective property in the object. It is without a concept; it is free of rules, procedures and purposes. But there is, nevertheless, some sort of quality in the representation of organization, a kind of fitting wholeness to the object or scene. This structure is there in the object, although it can only be recognized as beautiful once pleasure brings it to the fore of consciousness. Remember, without pleasure, beauty is nothing.

We will see a bit more about how this works in the next section on the final moment in Kant's analysis. We have laid all the groundwork for this moment, so the analysis will be short.

Fourth Moment: Necessary Delight

Here is the definition that Kant offers of this moment: 'The beautiful is that which, apart from a concept, is cognised as an object of necessary delight.' (1790) As we have established, when we see something as beautiful we think that others will experience the same kind of delight, and are disappointed when they do not. This means that we think of our experience as necessary in some sense. What can it mean that the beautiful is understood to be a *necessary* delight? And if delight is not necessary for everyone, how can it be classed as *necessary*?

Kant says that there must be a mental organization in us that, when properly functioning, responds with pleasure in the presence of certain organizational structures or patterns:

> *'[Judgements of taste] must have a subjective principle, and one that determines what pleases or displeases, by means of feelings only and not through concepts, and yet with universal validity. Such a principle, however, could only be regarded as a common sense [...] The judgement of taste, therefore, depends upon us presupposing the existence of a common sense.'* (1790)

'Common sense' here means that we assume that everyone has a certain common set of cognitive characteristics. Certain forms like the complicated intertwining of the lines upon a leaf prompt a feeling of pleasure, and we think that others should feel the same way. We are therefore supposing that everyone has a similar set of mental characteristics; that we are a community of similarly minded beings. As evidence for this, we attempt to communicate our appreciation of certain things by judgements of beauty and we think others will understand.

In order to understand this, let us go back to those purely rational beings. These beings have no feelings and so, although they see the same shapes and geometrical configuration, they feel nothing in response. Their responsive faculties cannot, therefore, be the same as ours. They certainly see that the Lake District has hills, rivers and cottages which are made up of lines and shapes. But they are puzzled when a human being says that the pattern of such things is beautiful. They see the configuration but not the pattern. They somehow do not notice the 'just rightness', since for them there is no pleasure to mark it. Whereas for those of us who can appreciate beauty, somehow we see not just a configuration but a *pattern or organization* that resonates with our faculties in an unconstrained, rule-free way. This results in feelings of delight. We do not ask, 'What is it for?' We just let the delight wash over us with a sense of wonder that things can be this way for us.

The Sublime

Kant talks a great deal about a different kind of aesthetic response – the sublime. As we saw in Chapter 2, Edmund Burke was a major influence on Kant's theories of the beautiful and the sublime. For Burke, these two notions are in direct contrast with one another. The sublime is *not* the beautiful. The beautiful is *not* the sublime. They are seen as two very different kinds of aesthetic response.

So what is the sublime? The sublime is when an experience of something overwhelms and floods the mind to overflowing. It cannot be taken in all at once. It cannot, says Kant, be comprehended. The typical example is the sight of a raging storm. The dark clouds glower and tumble chaotically. The outrageous roar of the wind makes the trees bend. The sudden violence of the lightning leaves the watcher awestruck. You feel acute discomfort and realize that this is beyond the bounds of your ability to comprehend, and this gives you a painful sense of smallness and inadequacy. Another example we can consider is the sea. The vastness of the ocean gives the sense of smallness and insignificance. The mighty movements of its surface and its overwhelming power cannot be tamed by categories and comprehension.

Kant distinguishes between two experiences of the sublime. One he identifies as to do with the mind's smallness and its inability to take it all in. Kant calls this experience of relative smallness 'the mathematical sublime' since it is to do with magnitude (the multiplication of units or measurement). The size or extent of the thing defies the ability to be viewed all at once. The other is to do with the power and might of the storm or the sea. Here you feel that the storm or sea completely defies your will. You cannot do anything about it. You are helpless in the face of such overwhelming power. The awe-inspiring might or power gives the 'dynamical sublime'.

So far we have talked about the displeasure or pain that the sight of the sea or storm gives. But of course it also gives pleasure. The ocean's might, combined with the force and magnitude of the storm, excites and repels. Kant agrees with Burke that you must be at a relatively safe distance from the storm to appreciate this. Actual fear would destroy the pleasure. No one in real danger of drowning in a stormy sea finds the experience sublime!

Kant says that you shake as you are attracted and crane forward eagerly, only to be flung back as the experience overwhelms. The experience is exciting, thrilling. This is presumably why people go on roller coasters or watch horror films. They want to experience something akin to the power of the sublime. It is a curious combination of pain and discomfort and thrill and excitement.

Compare the experience of the sublime with the beauty of a rose. The experience is very different. The beautiful seems more organized. The form or pattern is there and can be taken in. It does not overwhelm. The experience does not outrage the senses and the comprehension. It is altogether a much safer, contained experience.

That is not to say that a rose cannot be sublime. Imagine that you are able to look more closely at the rose – your eye able to discriminate further and further into its depths. No matter how far down you go there is more. The endless depth of the rose's microscopic detail now might prompt feelings of the sublime since now you realize that this simple rose is actually well beyond the comprehension of any finite individual. (This would be an example of the mathematical sublime.)

Kant distinguishes between the two types of sublime because he thinks that they teach us different things. He asks why both kinds of experience are pleasurable. They should, by all rights, only be painful. Why exactly should the sight of a storm thrill us? Why do we crane forward as we watch the film *Alien* (1979)? It should appal and revolt us with its chaotic, horrifying violence. And yet we find the sublime ennobling, pleasurable, thrilling, exciting, and awe-inspiring. Why is this?

The Mathematical Sublime

With the mathematical sublime, we cannot take the whole thing in. It is too big to be comprehended without losing the detail. It would be like looking at a storm from a great distance – now it is contained in one view, but the detail of the lightning hitting the tree is lost. The thrill is gone. So how does being in the middle of something incomprehensible thrill us? Kant's answer is somewhat surprising.

He notes that the mind does indeed desire or seek to take it all in, as the very notion that there is a totality here shows us that we are rational beings. We want to be thrilled by nature, but we also want to tame it in the sense of having an overall and comprehensive understanding.

We know from the other *Critiques* that Kant believes that we are beings with our feet in two realms. We are in the world of phenomena – the ordinary, empirical world of space, time, cause and effect. But we are super-sensible beings as well, or at least we have to assume we are. It is our noumenal selves – the pure rationality – at the heart of each one of us, which seeks to tame the storm. Our rationality wants to surround it with the over-arching noumenal self. For Kant, the storm is not sublime in itself. It serves to remind us of our transcendent, rational selves – the selves who seek to understand and comprehend it all.

Furthermore, says Kant, it reminds us that we are made in God's image whose omniscience does comprehend the storm. We are trying, in a sense, to emulate the infinite comprehension of the divine within the small compass of the finite human mind. We reach and clamour for the divine perspective. This is the sublime pleasure at the heart of the mathematical sublime.

The Dynamical Sublime

Our experiences testify, not to the greatness of the storm (that would just be terrifying) but to the way that we can defy the powers of the laws of nature. Remember that Kant believes that people are ends-in-themselves. The buck stops with us since we can begin an action that was not caused by something outside of ourselves. That is why we are responsible. The defying power of the storm or the sea reminds us that we are beings that have the tremendous power to act. We are not merely clockwork, causal beings. We are super-beings who have a special, awe-inspiring place in an overall noumenal reality which encompasses the phenomenal realm in which we live our lives. Just over our shoulders another realm lies where we are, like the storm, powerful, majestic and absolutely free.

In Summary

The beautiful reminds us that we are part of the universe. The beautiful is mysterious since it is non-conceptual, but it does not overwhelm. In that sense it is comprehensible and has form. Here is pleasure: it is safe and comforting; it can be homely. The sublime has a greater message – the world that we call home is part of a greater reality. Here there is a thrilling, awe-inspiring delight because the sublime reminds us that the phenomenal world is just one room in the vast mansion of the divine – a transcendent, noumenal mansion which is our eventual home and where we can finally and completely belong.

Conclusion

Having looked at Kant's key theories, we shall now consider some criticisms that have been made against his ideas. This, of course, will not be exhaustive. The aim is to let the interested reader know *some* of the main critical responses to Kant's ideas. Naturally there are Kantian responses to each of these criticisms, but that will have to be for the reader to explore in further study.

Let us look at one of the criticisms that has been made of the first *Critique*. We saw there that Kant divided reality into an experienced realm (the phenomenal world) and the noumenal world – the 'world as it is in itself' – which is necessarily always beyond human experience (see Chapter 3). Many critics have found this fundamental divide problematic. How can this utterly alien, non-spatial and non-temporal realm do anything? Recall it is somehow the foundation of the experiences that we have. How exactly can it be the foundation if it is, as Kant would have it, so utterly different from the world we actually experience? Kant thinks of the noumenal realm as non-temporal and non-spatial, but given that it is beyond human experience can we even know that?

In the second *Critique* we saw that, in some way, each person has roots in this other realm (see Chapter 4). We are, after all, also things in ourselves, so we too are part of this noumenal plane. However, we cannot experience it because everything knowable, including the experience of ourselves, is part of the empirical world. This implies a kind of fundamental unknowability at the heart of each person – a kind of empirical blank. Everyone as they are 'in themselves' is beyond empirical investigation. Some have seen this as a profound insight into the mystery of life, but others have thought it as introducing an unwelcome and unacceptable, non-scientific mysticism.

The idea of the noumenal realm provides Kant with the conceptual resources to leave room for radical human freedom. As we saw, in the phenomenal realm, we are subject to the organizing matrix of cause and effect. Considered as empirical beings we are subject to the necessitating pronouncements of physical law. But considered as an inhabitant of the noumenal realm we can understand ourselves to be free. We can choose in the radical 'buck stops here' sense that we examined in Chapter 4. We can be 'above' the otherwise compelling forces of appetite and desire, and make sovereign decisions based only upon reason. The idea of noumenal seems to be doing a lot of work here, and yet it is meant to be unknowable, and beyond empirical investigation. Can Kant be so sure that as noumenal beings we are free? Is this just a romantic fantasy?

Kant's account of morality has also come under fire. We have mentioned the worry that his account is perhaps unduly unemotional and dry. It seems that if we enjoy doing good deeds we are somehow in danger of performing actions that are without any moral worth. A passionate morality seems a contradiction in terms for Kant and yet many have complained, if we cannot get passionate about injustices and suffering then what can we get passionate about? Is a dry morality really morality as we understand it at all? Has Kant mistaken the fundamental nature of what it is to lead a moral life and replaced it with a bunch of dry, inhuman and implacable demands?

The absolute or categorical nature of Kant's ethical theory has provided critics with plenty of ammunition. Recall, for Kant, there is an absolute ban upon lying. No matter how appalling the consequences, lying is always absolutely impermissible since its maxim flies in the face of reason and 'annuls itself'. However, there seems to be plenty of circumstances where lying seems permissible. Indeed, there seem to be circumstances where lying is positively demanded. The infamous axe man at the door provides a vivid example of the morality of lying. In this scenario we are invited to think that a mad axe murderer arrives at your doorstep and asks where a friend of yours is hiding. You know that your friend is cowering upstairs. You also know that this man is intending to kill your friend. Do you tell the truth? Or do you lie saying that you have no idea where the potential victim is?

Kant sticks to his guns here and says that, even in these circumstances. it is wrong to lie. But this seems wildly implausible to most people. Surely lying here is permitted. We can modify the example where it appears even more obvious that lying is not always wrong. In this other scenario the person answering the door is hiding Jews from the murderous regime of the Nazis, and is asked by a member of the Gestapo if any Jewish people are hiding in the house. It seems utterly crazy to say that, in such circumstances, we cannot lie. Surely here we have a positive duty to lie, which is of course the exact opposite of what Kant says.

Finally let's turn to Kant's account of beauty (in Chapter 5). We saw that Kant puts quite severe restrictions upon what counts as a proper judgement about beauty. We need to be disinterested. We need to be free in the sense that we must not put the beautiful object under some concept. We must see it as organized in a certain way without going on to think of how that organization could be used. Some have questioned if there is enough left of the concept of beauty. Kant seems to have drained the idea of its lifeblood and then asked us to consider it vibrant and healthy. It all seems too formal, too abstract.

Remember, for example, the Kantian contrast between the trained botanist's judgements about flowers and the one who knows nothing of biology. The former, he says, is in danger of conceptualizing the flower while the latter is meant to somehow have a much more pure and unsullied delight. But many have noted that appreciation of beauty is often enhanced by knowledge, not ruined. Surely the botanist gets more and more entranced by the flower as she explores its nature in more and more depth. Her appreciation grows and the delight is more profound. She now knows why that does that and why that is there. There seems to be more and more appreciation of the beauty and yet, for Kant, it seems the expert botanist's appreciation of beauty shrinks as she explores different dimensions of how the flower works as a biological unit.

There are, of course, Kantian answers to all these problems (and there are a whole host of other criticisms that we might have mentioned). The debates go on. Kant's legacy and influence goes on. But one thing is certain, Kant is one of the most important philosophers ever to have lived and his ideas have changed the landscape of thinking in the Western world.

Bibliography

Works by Kant

Kant, I (1781) *Critique of Pure Reason* (revised edition 1787).

Kant, I (1783) *Prolegomena to any Future Metaphysics that Shall Come Forth as Scientific.*

Kant, I (1785) *Groundwork of the Metaphysics of Morals.*

Kant, I (1788) *Critique of Practical Reason.*

Kant, I (1790) *Critique of Judgement.*

Other works cited

Beck, Lewis (1969) *Early German Philosophy.* Cambridge: Harvard University Press.

Buckley, Paul and Peat, David F. (1979) *A Question of Physics: Conversations in Physics and Biology.* Toronto: University of Toronto Press.

Burke, Edmund (1757) *A Philosophical Enquiry into the Sublime and the Beautiful.* London: Penguin Books (this edition 1998).

Chigwell, Andrew (2009) '"As Kant has Shown" Analytic Theology and the Critical Theology' in Oliver D. Crisp and Michael C Rea (eds.) *Analytic Theology: New Essays in the Philosophy of Theology.* Oxford: Oxford University Press.

Hume, David (1748) *An Enquiry Concerning Human Understanding*, (ed.) Tom Beauchamp. Oxford: Oxford University Press (this edition 1999).

Rousseau, Jean-Jacques (1755) *A Discourse on Inequality*. London: Penguin Books (this edition 1984).

Rousseau, Jean-Jacques (1755) *A Discourse on Political Economy*. London: Penguin Books (this edition 2008).

Rousseau, Jean-Jacques (1762) *Of the Social Contract and Other Political Writings*. London: Penguin Books (this edition 2012).

Rousseau, Jean-Jacques (1762) *Émile: or On Education*. London: Penguin Books (this edition 1991).

Scruton, Roger (1982) *Kant*. Oxford: Oxford University Press.

Select Recommended Reading

Burnham, Douglas (2000) *An Introduction to Kant's 'Critique of Judgement'*. Edinburgh: Edinburgh University Press.

Beck, Lewis (1960) *A Commentary on Kant's 'Critique of Practical Reason.'* Chicago: University of Chicago Press.

Cassirer, Ernst (1945) *Rousseau Kant Goethe*. Princeton: Princeton University Press.

Ewing, A. C. (1938) *A Short Commentary on Kant's 'Critique of Pure Reason'*. Chicago: University of Chicago Press.

Körner, S (1955) *Kant*. London: Penguin Books.

Strawson, Peter (1966) *The Bounds of Sense: An Essay on Kant's 'Critique of Pure Reason'*. London: Methuen and Co.

Wenzel, Christian Helmut (2005) *An Introduction to Kant's Aesthetics: Core Concepts and Problems*. Oxford: Blackwell Publishing.

Biography

Mark Ian Thomas Robson received his PhD from Durham University. This was subsequently published by Continuum Press as *Ontology and Providence in Creation: Taking Ex Nihilo Seriously* (2008). Since then he has written a number of articles in various journals. His latest one was published in the *Royal Institute of Philosophy* journal and explored the account of free will given by Henri Bergson. Mark Robson teaches at a large comprehensive in Tyne and Wear, England.

Picture Credits:

jpg), „Christoph Bernhard Francke - Bildnis des Philosophen Leibniz (ca. 1695)", marked as public domain, more details on Wikimedia Commons: https://commons.wikimedia.org/wiki/ Template:PD-old. **Fig. 11** 'Jean-Jacques Rousseau (1712–78)'. Maurice Quentin de La Tour creator QS:P170,Q314655 (https://commons.wikimedia.org/wiki/File:Jean-Jacques_Rousseau_ (painted_portrait).jpg), „Jean-Jacques Rousseau (painted portrait)", marked as public domain, more details on Wikimedia Commons: https://commons.wikimedia.org/wiki/Template:PD-old. **Fig. 12** 'Edmund Burke (1729–97)'. Studio of Joshua Reynolds (https://commons.wikimedia. org/wiki/File:EdmundBurke1771.jpg), „EdmundBurke1771", marked as public domain, more details on Wikimedia Commons: https://commons.wikimedia.org/wiki/Template:PD-old.

Who the hell is

This exciting new series of books sets out to explore the life and theories of the world's leading intellectuals in a clear and understandable way. The series currently includes the following subject areas:

Art History | Psychology | Philosophy | Sociology | Politics

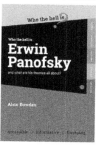

For more information about forthcoming titles in the Who the hell is...? series, go to: **www.whothehellis.co.uk**.

If any of our readers would like to put in a request for a particular intellectual to be included in our series, then please contact us at **info@whothehellis.co.uk**.

Printed in Great Britain
by Amazon

38473471R00078